# If You Want God to Help You Be at Peace…

DERRICK R. RHODES

PRESS

*If You Want God to Help You Be at Peace…*
by Derrick R. Rhodes

Printed in the United States of America

ISBN 9781612154473

www.xulonpress.com

In honor of Kelley Chapel United Methodist Church,
Mrs. Barbara Derrico, Mrs. Grace Fain, and Mrs. Eloise Miller

# CONTENTS

# HOW TO BE AT PEACE

**PURPOSE:** To teach you that God wants you to be at peace.

**READ SCRIPTURE:** Mark 5:1-6

They came to the other side of the lake, to the country of the Gerasenes. And when he had stepped out of the boat, immediately a man out of the tombs with an unclean spirit met him. He lived among the tombs; and no one could restrain him any more, even with a chain; for he had often been restrained with shackles and chains, but the chains he wrenched apart, and the shackles he broke in pieces; and no one had the strength to subdue him.

Night and day among the tombs and on the mountains he was always howling and bruising himself with stones. When he saw Jesus from a distance, he ran and bowed down before him;

NRSV

H ave you heard about Tracy Lyperd? Tracy was a beauty queen in Virginia a few years ago. Shortly after crowning her successor, she drove 250 miles to seek revenge on her ex-boy-friend for breaking up with her and marrying another woman. She took along a pistol, a hammer, lighter fluid, and matches. When she arrived at his house she got out of her car, walked up to the house, and rang the doorbell; it was answered by his new father-in-law.

Tracy faked having car trouble and asked the homeowner if she could use the telephone. After entering the house, she took out her hammer and hit the father-in-law on the head. She stunned him but didn't knock him out. What she didn't realize was that he was an ex-Secret Service agent. He grabbed her, and as they struggled and fought she pulled out the pistol from her purse and tried to shoot him. That's when the mother-in-law joined the fight and the two of them wrestled Tracy to the floor, holding her until the police arrived. When questioned, she said that she was driven to seek revenge because she needed "inner peace."

Multitudes of people from every walk of life, from Virginia to Vermont, from Florida to New York, from Mississippi to Maine, do not have inner peace. When they are alone they have their heads buried in their hands crying. A whole host of people, whether they are rich or poor, black or white, Jew or Gentile, are troubled. They are not mentally at peace; they are not spiritually at peace; they are constantly filled with stress and problems and pain. Why?

A ninety-five-year-old woman at the nursing home received a visit from one of her fellow church members.

"How are you feeling?" the visitor asked.

"Oh," said the lady, "I'm just worried sick!"

"What are you worried about, dear?" her friend asked. "You look rather well and healthy today. Are they taking good care of you here?"

"Oh, yes, they're taking very good care of me."

"Are you in any pain?" she asked.

"No, I'm not in any pain at all."

"Well, then what are you worried about?" her friend asked again.

The lady leaned back in her rocking chair, sighed a heavy sigh, and slowly explained her major worry. "Every close friend I ever had has already died and gone on to heaven. I'm afraid they're all wondering where I went."

Some people are not at peace. The shock and tremors of worry are wreaking havoc in their lives. They worry too much about what other people think, constantly stressing out because of this. "What are people thinking about me?" "What are people saying about me?"

Some people do what is right—treat people fairly, treat people like they want to be treated—not because they think it is right but because others think it is right. It is like they have not grown up out of their teenage years of peer pressure. Some people have become so caught up in what other people think of them that they are traumatized; they have literally lost themselves. They have become so caught up in what other people think that the result has been living with a boatload of fears, which are nothing but a deathtrap to their hopes and dreams:

- fear of being rejected
- fear of being thought a failure
- fear of making a mistake
- fear of being inferior
- fear of being seen as dumb

Quite a few people are not at peace because other people's voices are amplified in their head. They don't value their own opinion, their interpretation of what is being said, and what action needs to be taken.

A man decides to join the circus. He shows up to demonstrate his skills to the circus master.

"I have the most unusual act," he announces. "I'm sure it will amaze you." He proceeds to climb a tall tower and jump off. He flaps his arms wildly and then his fall slows. He soars forward, swoops upward, turns, and swoops back again. Finally he stops in midair and gently lowers himself to the ground, landing softly on the toe of one foot. The circus master stares at him blankly for a long time and finally says, "Is that all you've got? Bird imitations?"

For some people, nothing seems to satisfy them. They are always disgruntled. Whatever anyone does is never enough. They always have to have more: more clothes, more shoes, more food, more houses, more cars. And this more and more has become detrimental to them.

In this sometimes crude and cruel world, people everywhere are on a quest for peace. And there is all kinds of advice out there about how to obtain peace. The world is engulfed, inundated, with guidance for procuring tranquility of the soul. Listen to some of the advice.

- if you're feeling stressed, get the doctor to give you a prescription
- if your relationship is a struggle, end it with a divorce
- if you feel overwhelmed, buy something—new car, new shoes, new suit, new dress
- if you feel guilty, keep searching until you find someone who tells you that you aren't doing anything wrong
- if someone is tormenting you, get a gun and shoot them

Some people are not at peace because they get the wrong advice, and they implement that advice in their lives without even thinking it through. They are listening to the wrong people giving them the wrong counsel and inappropriate actions to take. What sense does it make to listen to someone give you advice about peace when he himself does not have peace? Would you get out in the middle of the ocean and let someone teach you how to swim when he does not know how to swim himself? Then why take advice about inner peace from someone who is clearly confused and befuddled, someone who doesn't know how to make sound decisions himself?

Let me show you something. In John 14:27, Jesus says, "Peace I leave with you; my peace I give to you. I do not give to you as the world gives. Do not let your hearts be troubled, and do not let them be afraid." (NRSV)) In John 20:19-21, we hear these words:

> When it was evening on that day, the first day of the week, and the doors of the house where the disciples had met were locked for fear of the Jews, Jesus came and stood among them and said, "Peace be with you."
>
> After he said this, he showed them his hands and his side. Then the disciples rejoiced when they saw the Lord. Jesus said to them again, "Peace be with you. As the Father has sent me, so I send you." (NRSV)

God wants us to have peace: peace in our mind, peace in our spirit, peace in our health. He wants us to have peace. And He knows how to help us have peace. After all, His Son is called the Prince of Peace. After all, God Himself created peace. After all, His Son said He was leaving us peace. Herb Miller tells this story about Thomas Carlyle:

> Thomas Carlyle was dressed to go out for a Sunday speech before a large crowd. His mother was sitting beside the front door. As Carlyle passed her on his way out, she said to him, "And where might you be going, Thomas?"
>
> "Mother," he replied, "I'm going to tell the people what is wrong with the world."

His mother responded with, "Aye, Thomas, but are you going to tell them what to do about it?" (*The Vital Church Leader*, Nashville: Abingdon Press, 1990, p.13)

## STOP HURTING YOURSELF

If you are not at peace, if your soul is troubled, God tells you what to do about it in Mark 5. Verse 5 of this chapter says, "Night and day among the tombs and on the mountains he was always howling and bruising himself with stones." Night and day this man roamed through the graves and hills screaming out and slashing himself with sharp stones. (NRSV)

You want to do wonders for your soul, to be at peace? You have to stop hurting yourself. You have to stop bruising yourself. Some of us have scars on our psyche—a scarred personality, a scarred self-image—because we put the scar there, not a friend, not a parent; we did it. You want peace of mind? Then stop hurting yourself, which is called self-inflicted pain. How do you do that?

Dig in your heels and stop putting yourself down. Some people are their own worst enemy. They keep putting themselves down. They keep telling themselves what they can't do and the reasons they can't do it. "I am too old." "I am too young." "I don't have enough money." Does that sound familiar?

Don't you know you are hurting yourself when you make these types of negative statements? How do you expect to be what God wants you to be when you continue to denigrate, degrade, and malign yourself? How do you expect to reach your full potential in this life when you allow negativity to creep into your soul?

We are so used to pessimistic feedback that we are more conscious of our weaknesses than our strengths. The Word of God says that you can do all things through Christ who strengthens you. That is what God says about you and that is what you can do if you would just stop being so negative about yourself. Stop putting yourself down! This is an integral part of obtaining peace.

John 8:32 gives us another answer about how to stop hurting yourself; hear what it says: "You will know the truth, and the truth will make you free." (NRSV) Irrespective of their age, disciples are learners. Their object is to know the truth. The way to know the truth is to obey the truth. Then and only then will the truth set you free.

The gospel obeyed frees. Frees us from what?

- Frees us from the yoke of Satan
- Frees us from selfishness
- Frees us from disobedience to God
- Frees us from fear and fills the soul with hope

To stop hurting yourself, you have to face the truth. There may be some things in your life that you know you need to stop doing. Or there may be some things in your life that you need to start doing. You have told yourself that and other people have told you too. You just need to face the truth and do it. Someone said, "Just remember, you can do anything you set your mind to, but it takes action, perseverance, and facing fears."

Don't focus on your weaknesses. Every person has weaknesses, but focusing on them is an ill-fated strategy. Invariably focus on your strengths. Focus on what you do well. To be at peace, you have to stop hurting yourself. Say to yourself, "I am going to stop taking cheap shots at myself. Enough of the putdowns."

## CONTROL

Mark 5:2-3 has a powerful message about being at peace: "And when he had stepped out of the boat, immediately a man out of the tombs with an unclean spirit met him. He lived among the tombs; and no one could restrain him anymore, even with a chain." (NRSV)

What was controlling this man? The text says unclean spirits. The New International Version says an evil spirit. In verse 9 (look at it) Jesus asks this man his name and the man responds "Legion." The man was telling us something about himself when he called himself Legion. What was he telling us?

Well, a legion is six thousand soldiers. So I believe, as some biblical scholars do, that this man was saying he was filled with multiple demons. For the people of Palestine, hemmed in by occupied forces, a legion—whether spiritual or human—struck terror! This man was being controlled and managed by multiple unclean spirits, multiple evil spirits, multiple foreign entities.

Paul Harvey told a story about a lady who was overweight and blamed it on the traffic on the city street. She would go to bed at night and the traffic outside her window would keep her awake. So, rather than lie there awake, she'd get up and eat. Her reason for being overweight wasn't her overeating or a physical problem she had, but rather the traffic. This lady's attitude applies to so many of us. We allow too many outside forces to control us. We allow too many outside forces to have power over us—to be in command of our mindset and our posture.

To be at peace, to rid yourself of that inner intensity, not only do you have to stop hurting yourself but you also have to get control of your life. You have to get a handle on things. You can't allow these multiple outside forces—friends, material things, deadlines—to control you. You can't keep allowing yourself to be driven and manipulated daily by exterior energies that leave you spiritually destitute, spiritually malnourished.

What are some things you can do to help get control of your life? To control your life you have to know what your values are. What do I mean? I mean you have to know what you believe. Why?

You have to know what you believe because if you don't you will fall for anything. If you don't know what you believe—what your values are—you will take up any cause, any project, any mission, any assignment. And before you know it you will have too much on your plate—some things you like and a whole lot of things you don't like.

And what is the aftermath of a plate that is full of things you like and a whole lot of things you don't like? Confusion, unrest, turmoil, chaos, mayhem, and weeds of bitter discontent. To control your life you have to know what your values are. You have to ask yourself questions like: What is important to me? Who is important to me? So know what you value. Know what you believe. Know what is important to you.

The other thing I would suggest is this. Ask yourself, "What am I enslaved to?" Food? Lust? Power? Money? The past? Drugs? Alcohol? Jealousy? Anger? Fill in the blank. Then ask yourself, "What do I have to say no to at this very moment? What do I have to say yes to at this very moment?"

Another thing you have to have is self-discipline. Author H. Jackson Brown was right when he said, "Talent without discipline is like an octopus on roller skates. There's plenty of movement, but you never know if it's going to be forward, backwards, or sideways." When you don't have self-discipline, you are all over the place. You are into everything. That's what you call muddled, mixed-up, confused. You have to have self-discipline if you are going to control your life and have peace.

Listen to what Tiger Woods said: "I think the guys who are really controlling their emotions...are going to win." He is right is he? Because he didn't control his emotions, he is really losing now.

Our text, Mark 5:1-6, tells us in verse 6 that when this man possessed with unclean spirits saw Jesus, he ran to Jesus and bowed down before Him. And after a brief dialogue between this man and Jesus, Jesus heals the man. As a result the man who had an unclean spirit finds the peace he had been looking for all his life. He was no longer hurting himself. He was in control of his life. Do you want peace? Then do what this man did: bring whatever is disturbing you to Jesus.

Don't keep holding onto it. Don't keep trying to overcome it by yourself. Don't keep trying to conquer it with the world's remedies. Bring whatever it is to Jesus. He has been waiting for you to bring it to Him. Let go of it and let Him have it.

For you see, if you don't let go of it you will constantly give into defeat. If you don't let go of it you will always feel down-in-the-dumps. If you don't let go of it you will continue to have negative thoughts.

Whatever it is, bring it to Jesus and let it go. Let Him help bring you peace of mind. Let Him help you restore your confidence. Let Him help you rebuild your crushed life. Let Him help you renew your heart's desire. Let Him help you repair your ruined relationship.

Whatever it is, do like this man in our text and bring it to Jesus. He is the only One who can provide for your needs. He is the only One who can satisfy your longings. He is the only One who can comfort your heart.

Bring it to Him right now. Don't hold onto it any longer. Bring it to Him right now.

- He is the only One who can give you peace of mind that passes all understanding.
- He is the only One who can inspire your hopes.
- He is the only One who can be your bridge over troubled waters.
- He is the only One who can calm your nerves.
- He is the only One who can bring you out of darkness into His marvelous light.
- He is the only One who can put a spring back into your step.
- He is the only One who can remove the loneliness from your heart.
- He is the only One who can plant your feet on solid ground.
- He is the only One who can deliver you from the fiery furnace.
- He is the only One who can give you victory day after day.
  - Whatever it is, bring it to Him and watch Him cast it out.
  - Bring it to Him and watch Him fix it.
  - Bring it to Him and watch Him give you the victory.
  - Bring it to Him and watch Him make it right.
  - Bring it to Him and watch Him sort it out.

     o   Bring it to Him and watch Him give you the cure.

     o   Bring it to Him and watch Him give you the answer.

Don't hold onto it—your hurts, your frustrations, your worries—any longer. Do like this man in the text. Bring it to Jesus and let it go.

# CHAPTER ONE

# COPING WITH CHANGES

**PURPOSE:** To teach you that whatever change you are going through you can handle it if you know how.

**READ SCRIPTURE:** Matthew 8:28-34

When he came to the other side, to the country of the Gadarenes, two demoniacs coming out of the tombs met him. They were so fierce that no one could pass that way. Suddenly they shouted, "What have you to do with us, Son of God? Have you come here to torment us before the time?" Now a large herd of swine was feeding at some distance from them. The demons begged him, "If you cast us out, send us into the herd of swine." And he said to them, "Go!" So they came out and entered the swine; and suddenly, the whole herd rushed down the steep bank into the lake and perished in the water. The swineherds ran off, and on going into the town, they told the whole story about what had happened to the demoniacs. Then the whole town came out to meet Jesus; and when they saw him, they begged him to leave their neighbourhood. (NRSV)

I remember about eighteen years ago when I pastored Bethel UMC, my son, Sentelle, and I were on our way to pick up my wife from somewhere. Well, I stopped by the church to call her to let her know we were running late but were on our way. I gave Sentelle my key and told him to go into the church kitchen and call his mother and tell her we were on the way. After about ten minutes of him being inside the church, I started saying to myself, "What is taking him so long?"

So I went to check on him. When I strolled into the kitchen, I saw him standing over the phone staring at it. I said, "What is taking you so long?"

He replied, "I don't know how to use the phone."

I said, "You don't know how to use the phone?"

And he looked at me with tears in his eyes, shaking his head. The phone he was trying to use was a rotary dial, and he had never used one before. Can you believe that? He had never used a rotary dial phone before. He had only used a push button phone.

Life is full of changes. Things never really stay the same. We've gone from rotary phones to push button phones to cell phones.

I heard a story about a man who accepted the invitation to attend his twenty-fifth high school reunion by writing "I hope you'll recognize me...I've got the 5 B's...baldness, bifocals, bridgework, bulges, and bunions."

Life is always on the move. People change. Communities change. Governments change. Life, no matter how we try to manipulate it (and we do try to manipulate it), is vigorous and prone to change.

Some changes are expected, and some are unexpected; some are good, and some are not so good; some are a relief, and some are devastating. Life is full of changes whether we like it or not. Sometimes change is forced on us such as a full-time job being downsized to a part-time job, or going from being well to being sick. Life is full of changes.

Mark Twain said, "The only person who likes change is a wet baby." We might not be beguiled by change but whether we like it or not life is full of changes.

Change is inevitable — except, as someone has said, from vending machines. Other than that change is certain. I heard someone say if you are in a bad situation, don't worry, it will change; if you are in a good situation, don't worry, it will change. Change is inevitable.

What are some of our negative responses to change? Some people respond to change by quitting. They say, "If you change my job, if you change my position, if you change the way I do things, I just won't participate." Some people respond to change by staying in a down mood. They become lethargic, unresponsive, and spiritless. Lisa Beamer ruminates on the loss of her dad in her book *Let's Roll*.

Slowly I began to understand that the plans God has for us don't just include "good things", but the whole array of human events. The "prospering" he talks about in the book of Jeremiah is often the outcome of a "bad" event. I remember my mom saying that many people look for miracles—things that in their human minds "fix" a difficult situation. Many miracles, however, are not a change to the normal course of human events; they're found in God's ability and desire to sustain and nurture people through even the worst situations. Somewhere along the way, I stopped demanding that God fix the problems in my life and started to be thankful for his presence as I endured them. (Lisa Beamer: *Let's Roll: Ordinary People, Extraordinary Courage*. Tyndale House Publishers, 2002, p. 69.)

Some people respond to change by becoming wiser, more judicious in their approach to life's situations and circumstances. Other people respond to change by going into a state of denial: "This is not true…this is not happening…this is not happening to me."

Some people respond to change by getting angry. They become furious, their heart filled with resentment and a desire to get revenge against the person who has moved their cheese.

Someone once said, "Everybody is in favor of progress. It is the change they don't like." Some people respond to change by trying to stop the change, by trying to slow it down, by trying to bring it to a standstill, by trying to put an end to it.

Dr. Linda Ladd, Texas Cooperative Extension family development specialist, said:

> Life changes every day for every person in some way. We expect the seasons to change, children to grow taller, birthdays to keep piling on, strawberries in June and the crisp smell of fall in October...we expect to grow older...to watch children marry, to retire from our jobs and play with our grandchildren. ("Coping with Life's Changes," Agnews, News and Public Affairs.)

Change is inevitable, and we need to know how to handle it. Why? First of all, we need to know how to handle change because if we don't it will destroy us. Second, we need to know how to handle change because our children are watching us, and they learn how to handle change by seeing how we handle it.

The purpose of this lesson is to get you to see that whatever change you are going through you can handle it if you know how. Dr. Cara DiMarco, a counselor in Oregon and author of *Moving through Life Transitions with Power and Purpose*, says, "All major changes involve a component of loss at their center....That loss might involve loss of a particular routine, loss of opportunities, loss of a sense of yourself or a loss of hope." (Healthline: connect to better health)

Whatever change—age, job, marriage, health—you are going through in your life, you can cope with it if you know how. How do you cope with change?

## LETTING GO

Philippians 3:13 says, "Beloved I do not consider that I have made it my own way; but this one thing I do: forgetting what lies behind and straining forward to what lies ahead." (NRSV) Paul says that he forgets the past and looks forward to what lies ahead.

Up the street, near the funeral home on Candler Drive, I saw this quote on a church marquee: "Yesterday ended last night. Let go of it." To cope with change, let go of the past and move on. Some of us have been hurting, filled with anger, depressed, and restless not because of something we are dealing with in the present but because of something from the past.

Changes have happened or are happening in your life whether you want them or not, so it is befitting for you to stop looking back, stop clinging to the past. There's nothing wrong with remembering "the good old days"—the uplifting things about your past—but be careful because even those things can trip you up and keep you stuck in the past. To survive change, let go of the past—"the what-ifs and should-haves"—and move on. How do you let go of the past?

28

When the railroads were first introduced to the United States, some folks feared that they'd be the downfall of the nation! Here's an excerpt from a letter to then President Jackson dated January 31, 1829:

> As you may know, Mr. President, "railroad" carriages are pulled at the enormous speed of 15 miles per hour by "engines" which, in addition to endangering life and limb of passengers, roar and snort their way through the countryside, setting fire to crops, scaring the livestock and frightening women and children. The Almighty certainly never intended that people should travel at such breakneck speed. — Martin Van Buren, Governor of New York (sermonillustrations. com)

Just think how this world would be if there were no changes:

- African Americans would still be slaves.
- We would still be riding around on horses and donkeys.
- There would be no computers or emails or Facebook.
- There would be no cures to diseases.
- There would be no fresh experiences.
- We would not have a black president.

Without change, events in this world would be mundane, unexciting, uninteresting, and stale. We would not be able to exercise our freewill—our ability to choose that helps us to mature spiritually. To let go of the past, you need to know that change can be good; it can be beneficial; it can be advantageous.

To let go of the past, know that at first the change in your life may be devastating. You may become befuddled for a moment, but realize that you can move beyond it. It may be difficult to deal with at first, but you can make it through. You have to believe that because no one else—mother, father, husband, wife, children, friend, relative, Big Mama—can do it for you.

To let go of your past, don't be so set in your ways, thinking that if things don't work the way they have been that you are not going to do anything at all. You will sideline your life. Be adaptable, open-minded. Openness is basically the eagerness to grow, a disgust for ruts, and eagerly standing on tiptoes looking toward the future for a better picture of what tomorrow may bring.

Dr. Joan Borysenko, coauthor of *Saying Yes to Change*, said, "When you try to put your life in a box and keep it the same all the time, you're making something dead out of it.…People who greet what life offers with curiosity have stronger immune systems and live longer." (*Prevention* Magazine, July 2006)

Don't be so inflexible, having an uncompromising spirit. People who are like this can never let go of the past and move on to brighter days.

To let go of your past, decide that you are not going to be a victim. Be determined that you are not just going to lie down and stop trying because you don't like the things that are changing in your life.

Roger Staubach, who led the Dallas Cowboys to the World Championship in 1971, admitted that his position as a quarterback who didn't call his own signals was a source of trial for him. Coach Landry sent in every play. He told Staubach when to pass, when to run, and only in emergency situations could he change the play (and he had better be right!). Even though Staubach considered Coach Landry to have a "genius mind" when it came to football strategy, pride said that he should be able to run his own team. Staubach later said, "I faced up to the issue of obedience. Once I learned to obey there was harmony, fulfillment, and victory."

To let go of your past, decide that God is changing your life and you are going to be obedient and go in the new direction He is leading you. And when you do, let me tell you there will be harmony, there will be fulfillment, there will be victory for you!

## WHAT'S IMPORTANT

Matthew 8 tells us that when Jesus was in Gadarenes, he ran into two men possessed with demons. He healed these two men by casting the demons into a herd of pigs that were standing nearby, and the pigs took off running and ran off a steep bank into the sea and perished. You see the people's response to Jesus healing the "demoniacs" in verse 34: "Then the whole town came out to meet Jesus; and when they saw him, they begged him to leave their neighborhood." (NRSV)

Do you see what is going on here? These people were angry with Jesus about the pigs dying instead of being happy about the two men, whom some of them knew personally, being healed. They were more concerned about the filthy pigs than about God's precious people.

During a flood in the hill country of Texas in 1978 a lady lost her life needlessly. Her daughter told reporters, "My mother did not climb the tree with us. She lost her way before we got to the tree. See, she always kept every little bill and slip and stuff. She would not let go of her purse with those papers in it." It was revealed that the family was trying to make a chain, holding hands to get through the water. But the mother had her insurance papers all gathered up in her hands and wouldn't drop those documents. So she just washed away.

Maybe you have had some changes in your life recently. Do you know what you need to do now? Not run off and hide somewhere, not get angry (and it is a normal response to get angry for a moment, but you don't stay in this state of mind), not feel sorry for yourself, but decide what is important now. At this juncture in your life what is important? What is significant? What is essential? What is important to your bedrock, your care, your foundation?

Well, how do you do that? How do you decide what is important? For a lot of things may seem to be important, even essential, for us personally. What is important? What is essential for you at this moment in your life? How do you answer that question?

First of all, look at what you have now and what it will take to move your life in the direction you feel God is calling you to go. What is it going to take to get where you feel God is leading you? What is critical for you to survive now?

Second, develop some goals, things you want to accomplish in the days to come, and write your goals down. There is something about writing goals down on paper that causes us to more readily achieve them.

Third, chart your progress; that is, keep a journal of steps you have made toward achieving your goals. I believe this is necessary because like any journey—and your goals are a journey because you are going somewhere if you stick to them—if you don't check to see where you are along your journey you will never know when you have arrived or how far away you are from arriving, or you will miss your exit and never be able to celebrate the fact that you did arrive at your planned destination. And, believe me, celebrating your arrival at your planned destination is important.

It gives you hope and encouragement that you can fulfill your dreams, that God does have a purpose for your life, that God is watching over you and helping you to get where He is calling you to be. It converts your sadness into laughter. Deciding what is important for you now will help you to focus your energy.

- It will help you to have desire.
- It will help you to have determination.
- It will help you to have willpower to run your race regardless of what you face.

In Genesis 32:9-12 we hear these words:

And Jacob said, "O God of my father Abraham and God of my father Isaac, O LORD who said to me, 'Return to your country and to your kindred, and I will do you good', I am not worthy of the least of all the steadfast love and all the faithfulness that you have shown to your servant, for with only my staff I crossed this Jordan; and now I have become two companies. Deliver me, please, from the hand of my brother, from the hand of Esau, for I am afraid of him; he may come and kill us all, the mothers with the children. Yet you have said, 'I will surely do you good, and make your offspring as the sand of the sea, which cannot be counted because of their number.'" (NRSV)

How would you feel knowing that you were about to meet the person you had connived out of his most precious possession? Jacob had taken Esau's birthright and his blessings. Now he was about to meet face-to-face with his brother for the first time in twenty years, and he was frantically fearful. So what did he do? He collected his thoughts and decided to pray, which he should have done anyway before he stole his brother's birthright and blessings. But one of the things this story is about is God telling us to pray, and it's never too late to pray.

To cope with change not only do you have to decide what is important, you also have to pray about what God wants you to do next. Talk to God about your goals—(1) where He wants you to be, (2) what He wants you to do, (3) how He wants you to get there, (4) who you need to contact—that He wants you to focus on in the days ahead, specifically during the next ninety days and the next two to five years.

The next step is to get started. Don't delay; you have been delaying too long saying you will get started tomorrow—but have you noticed that this tomorrow you keep talking about has never come?

What do you need to know as you take this new journey? First of all, you may get stuck every now and then. You may get started but you may get stuck. Second, when that happens, write down the question that keeps popping up in your mind as to why you are stuck, why you are trapped, and then wait for God to give you an answer and show you what to do to get unstuck. Let God show you how to pull yourself out of the muck and miry clay.

Every summer, and two or three times during the year, we have a yard sale in our neighborhood. It's time for people to clean out their garages and closets and attics and storage spaces of things they no longer need, or things they bought and never opened or used. You know what I'm talking about: getting rid of the clutter. Sometimes we buy and accumulate so much stuff it makes our lives look disorderly and messy. And what do we do to relieve ourselves? We have a yard sale, praying that someone will come and take the clutter off our hands.

As you travel this journey, you are going to collect stuff you don't need—fear, hate, jealousy, envy, greed, selfishness, and meanness—and you are going to need to have a yard sale of your own life

- to get rid of those things that are hampering your life
- to purge yourself of some things that are slowing you down
- to free yourself of some things that are impeding your success

To cope with change, you have to pray about what God wants you to do next; then you have to get started and the result will be a new you, a you that is empowered and ready, willing and able to face the challenges, hopes, and dreams of tomorrow.

As you cope with any change that is going on in your life (and I assume that's why you bought this book), you will come up against some stuff that may take you for a loop, that may seek to tear you asunder, that may be too much for you to handle alone. But know that as you face these challenges—trials and tribulations, loneliness and despair, hardships and heartaches—there is no change that God cannot help you with.

Change is difficult. By no means am I saying that it is not. But what I am saying, what I do want you to know, is that it is not too difficult for God, who will help you with it if you let Him.

- To see you through, God is ready to do.
- To see you through, God is willing to do.
- To see you through, God is eager to do.

You may be hurt right now, but there is a new day around the corner; you just have to believe it is there and that God is going to help you obtain it. Prayers have been made to help you to make it. Tears have been shed to help you to make it. Testimonies have been given to help you to make it.

Your new day is just around the corner, and God is going to get you there. I know things are changing—changing every day—and people you used to trust you can't trust anymore. But know this: Things are changing in your life but God never changes. Gold prices change but not God. The stock market changes but not God. The weather is unpredictable but not God. The job market is extremely undependable but not God.

God is always ready and willing to help you. So stop trying to lift your burdens yourself. They are too heavy for you, too intense for you. But if you ask God, He'll help you with the change. He'll help you face your change if you trust Him.

- When worry grips you, trust Him.
- When stress paralyzes you, trust Him.
- When pressure immobilizes you, trust Him
- When aggravation plagues you, trust Him.

It's tough and it's rough, but God is ready and willing. All you have to do is ask Him for help and He will help you.

- Don't wait until your marriage falls apart before asking for help.
- Don't wait until the doctor shakes his head before asking for help.
- Don't wait until you suffer needlessly before asking for help.
- Don't wait until your family turns against you before asking for help.
- Don't wait until people start gossiping about you before asking for help.
- Don't wait until your future is pathetic before asking for help.

- Don't wait until you can't take it anymore before asking for help.
- Don't wait until the last moment before asking for help.
- Don't wait until you fall to pieces before asking for help.
- Don't wait until your life is almost over before asking for help.
  - o He promises to hear your prayer.
  - o He promises to supply your need.
  - o He promises to give you when you ask.
  - o He promises to open the door when you knock.
    - He's the Bread of life.
    - Hope for the hopeless.
    - Strength for the weak.

He will help you to cope with your change; all you have to do is ask, all you have to do is call on His name.

# CHAPTER TWO

# WHAT TO DO WITH YOUR HURTS

**PURPOSE:** To teach you to make the right decisions about your hurts.

**READ THE SCRIPTURE:** Job 23:10-17

But he knows the way that I take; when he has tested me, I shall come out like gold.
My foot has held fast to his steps; I have kept his way and have not turned aside.
I have not departed from the commandment of his lips; I have treasured in my bosom the words of his mouth.
But he stands alone and who can dissuade him?
What he desires, that he does.
For he will complete what he appoints for me; and many such things are in his mind.
Therefore I am terrified at his presence;
when I consider, I am in dread of him.
God has made my heart faint; the Almighty has terrified me; If only I could vanish in darkness, and thick darkness would cover my face! (NRSV)

Yesterday, after the tornadoes struck Alabama, a lady said that one minute everything was just fine and the next she was so hurt she couldn't finish her sentence. She just bowed her head in sorrow.

Our world is filled with hurting people; people who have been bruised because of the loss of a close friend; people who have been bruised because of the loss of a home—or everything they have; people whose hearts have been broken by someone they loved; people whose hearts have been shattered because of the loss of a leader.

I read that actor Denzel Washington was out with friends recently when a homeless man moved in to ask for money. The actor's entourage ignored the man in the hope that he would go away. But Washington noticed him and was touched by his unhappy plight. If we are any kind of Christian at all, we ought to be at least be touched by the pain and hurt of others.

An evangelist was riding on a plane filled with people, cigarette smoke, and defiled air. (Of course, this doesn't happen today.) The evangelist knew he would have to take a bath and send his clothes to the cleaners. He felt like he had been char-broiled. His chest and lungs were filled with smoke. Suddenly he turned to a woman and said, "Would you like to chew my gum for awhile?"

The lady was insulted. "What in the world do you mean?" she snapped.

The evangelist calmly replied, "I've been smoking your second-hand smoke ever since we left the city. I thought you might want my secondhand gum."

Some people are very insensitive to others. They may blow smoke in your face, open their car door in a parking lot and bang your car, throw their trash on the ground, cut you off in traffic, run a red light without regard for others, run through a door while you are holding it open for some elderly person. But these are not the worst insensitivities of them all. What's the worst insensitivity? The worst insensitivity of all is when someone is hurting badly and no one seems to care.

That homeless man who came up to Denzel Washington asking for money, the others in Denzel's entourage ignored him, but not Denzel. He noticed the man and was touched by his unhappy plight. What did he do? He reached into his pocked and handed him a $100 bill. The man began to cry. Soon after that he grabbed a passerby and said, "Will Smith just gave me a hundred bucks!" I doubt that Denzel Washington was offended by that remark if he heard about it.

There are a lot of hurting people in the world: the homeless, the unemployed, the hungry, the depressed, the deserted, the forgotten. The following poem demonstrates explicitly how hurting affects us:

My heart is breaking but you cannot tell

I put a smile on my face and speak as I will

Carrying on a conversation if you have the time

My heart is breaking and no one knows why

I am grieving because of the losses in my life

Parents never get over the death of a child

It hurts real bad when your parents are gone

Nothing compares to that child you hold so dear

He has gone on before me and I am so broken

How many people have I passed today that have a broken heart

It may not be the same reason as me, yet we keep on going

Hoping for the best in the people we see

I have come to realize that most people are hurting

Maybe not for the same reason but the pain is the same

My heart is breaking but I must go on, looking like I am happy

That way people will not feel sorry for me

I am a good actress because of the hurts

Pretending I am fine, when in fact my heart is breaking!!

(George and Sarah Berthelson)

A lot of people in this world could have written this poem. People from every race, every economic background, every community, every church, and every political party are hurting in some way.

The man in our text, whom everyone has heard about, was hurting. His name was Job. He was a righteous man who was faithful to God and lived a good and moral life. He was blessed with a good marriage, seven sons and three daughters, and much wealth and resources.

Job suffered a tragedy in which he lost almost everything in a few days. He lost all his wealth, and his children were all killed in what appears to have been a tornado. His health broke down; his body was afflicted with a painful skin disease; he was wounded; life had thrown him an excruciating body blow that knocked the wind out of him.

But what does Job do? Our text tells us in Job 23:10 that Job says, "He knows the way that I take, when he has tested me, I shall come forth like gold." (NRSV) Do you know what I hear God saying in this verse? I hear God saying, "Yes, you will be hurt in this life." Yes, life will wound each and every one of His children, but when that happens God wants us to make the right decision about our hurts. When we have been hurt—and we will at some point in time be hurt—God is very concerned about us taking the appropriate action. He wants us to make the right judgment about those hurts, those life afflictions, those misfortunes. He wants us to make the right choice.

## MAKING THE WRONG DECISION

Why does God want us to make the right decision about our hurts? A mother, hearing a startling scream from her four-year-old son, rushed into the playroom to see what was happening. There he sat while his baby sister yanked his hair with all her might. "Don't be upset," said his mother. "She doesn't know that it hurts you." Several minutes later, the mother again heard sharp screaming, this time from the little daughter. Once more in the playroom, she asked her son, "What's wrong with the baby?"

"Nothing much," he said, "except now she knows."

God is concerned about us making the right decisions when we are hurting because so many of us, seasoned saints and newly maturing saints, make the wrong decision when we are hurt. Many of us take the wrong actions. Some of us say the wrong things. Some of us do the wrong things.

## DESTRUCTIVE AND NEGATIVE INFLUENCE

But this is not the only reason why God is concerned. Mark 14:44-46 says:

> Now the betrayer had given them a sign, saying, "The one I will kiss is the man; arrest him and lead him away under guard." So when he came, he went up to him at once and said, "Rabbi!" and kissed him. Then they laid hands on him and arrested him. (NRSV)

Jesus had been predicting His destiny and death and telling His disciples about it along their journey together. But Judas was not pleased with the message Jesus was conveying, and perhaps he thought to himself, "Before this man called Jesus does something stupid—because he is talking crazy—I'm going to get something out of this deal. I gave up everything to follow this sucker."

Judas was obviously hurting because he expected more from Jesus than for Jesus just to allow Himself to be killed. So Judas brokers a deal with the Pharisees to identify Jesus for them for thirty pieces of silver. After Judas carries out his dirty deed, after the Pharisees capture Jesus, Judas begins to feel guilty because of what he has done and commits suicide.

What's my point? My point is this: If you make the wrong decision about your hurts, they can become a destructive and negative influence. If you are not careful, your hurts can destroy you. Over and over again they can keep hurting you. Not only that, but your hurts can cause you to hurt someone else.

## ABUNDANT LIFE

In his medical practice, Dr. Richard Swenson sees a steady stream of hurting people coming into his office. He claims that a majority of them suffer from a chronic ailment that has reached epidemic levels in our country. Do you know what it is? SARS maybe? Or AIDS?

The disease Dr. Swenson is concerned about is what he calls a lack of MARGIN. Margin is the space that once existed between us and our limits. It's something held in reserve for contingencies or unanticipated situations. As a society, we've forgotten what margin is. In the push for progress, margin has been devoured. We're overloaded.

Dr. Swenson describes the results of this kind of living. We feel distressed in ill-defined ways. We are besieged by anxiety, stress, and fatigue. Our relationships suffer. We have unexplained aches and pains. The flood of daily events seems beyond our control. Does that sound familiar? How different does that sound from the words of Jesus: "The thief comes only to steal and kill and destroy; I have come that you might have life, and have it to the full." (John 10:10 NIV).

God wants us to make the right decisions about our hurts because He wants us to have life and have it more abundantly. And our decisions about our hurts—our responses to the pains that life inflicts on us—can affect the abundant life He wants us to have. Well, what do we need to do about our hurts? Okay, I am going to tell you, but first let's take a look at what you don't do.

## A SWIFT, IRREVERSIBLY NEGATIVE DECISION

In Job 1:13-22 let's see what Job does *not* do. Watch this.

> One day when his sons and daughters were eating and drinking wine in the eldest brother's house, a messenger

came to Job and said, "The oxen were ploughing and the donkeys were feeding beside them, and the Sabeans fell on them and carried them off, and killed the servants with the edge of the sword; I alone have escaped to tell you."
While he was still speaking, another came and said, "The fire of God fell from heaven and burned up the sheep and the servants, and consumed them; I alone have escaped to tell you."

While he was still speaking, another came and said, "The Chaldeans formed three columns, made a raid on the camels and carried them off, and killed the servants with the edge of the sword; I alone have escaped to tell you."

While he was still speaking, another came and said, "Your sons and daughters were eating and drinking wine in their eldest brother's house, and suddenly a great wind came across the desert, struck the four corners of the house, and it fell on the young people, and they are dead; I alone have escaped to tell you." Then Job arose, tore his robe, shaved his head, and fell on the ground and worshipped. He said, "Naked I came from my mother's womb, and naked shall I return there; the LORD gave, and the LORD has taken away; blessed be the name of the LORD."

In all this Job did not sin or charge God with wrongdoing. (NRSV)

In all this craziness going on in Job's life, he could have done something really stupid. He could have made some unwise moves. But the text says that although he lost all his servants, although he lost all his livestock, although he lost all his children, he did not sin against God.

What am I saying to you? I am saying that whatever you do, don't make a swift, irreversibly negative decision when you are hurting. When you are hurting, you are not at your best. You are not as strong as you normally would be. When you are hurting, if you make a move right then and there, you are probably going to do something stupid—you are probably going to do something that doesn't make any sense.

I remember when I first started dating my wife, I brought her an engagement ring, and for some stupid reason that I can't even remember now, we got into an argument. I guess I was losing the argument so I asked for her to give me my ring back. I was so upset I was losing the argument, so upset that I was wrong and my wife was proving it, that I took that ring—that ring I had worked so hard to get the money to buy, and still owed money for, and threw it out in the field where we were standing at the time. After I realized what I had done, I ran desperately out into that field trying to find the ring. I want you to know—I never found it.

Whatever you do, don't make a swift, irreversibly negative decision when you are hurting. When you feel you have been bruised by someone you love, or bruised by life, you are not at your finest. You are not as wise as you usually would be. When you are hurt, if you make a move right at that moment, you are probably going to do something outlandish —something that doesn't make any sense.

## MAKING MATTERS WORSE

I had a friend who was hurt by a girl when we were in college, and he has been single to this day. I saw him recently and said, "Have you gotten married yet?"

"Man, you know I'm not going to get married," he said.

"Why?" I asked.

He said, "You know what that girl did to me?"

When you have been hurt, don't make matters worse. What am I saying? Some of us get hurt by one person, and we think the whole world is out to get us. Some man hurts you, and you think all men are bad. Some woman hurts you, and you think all women are bad. Some pastor hurts you, and you think all pastors are bad. Don't make matters worse than they are.

Farmer Joe decided his injuries from the accident were serious enough to take the trucking company (responsible for the accident) to court. In court, the trucking company's fancy lawyer was questioning Farmer Joe.

"Didn't you say, at the scene of the accident, I'm fine?" questioned the lawyer.

Farmer Joe responded, "Well, I'll tell you what happened. I had just loaded my favorite mule Bessie into the..."

"I didn't ask for any details," the lawyer interrupted, "just answer the question. Did you not say, at the scene of the accident, I'm fine!"

Farmer Joe said, "Well, I had just got Bessie into the trailer and I was driving down the road..."

The lawyer interrupted again and said, "Judge, I am trying to establish the fact that, at the scene of the accident, this man told the highway patrolman on the scene that he was just fine. Now several weeks after the accident he's trying to sue my client. I believe he is a fraud. Please tell him to simply answer the question."

By this time the judge was fairly interested in Farmer Joe's answer and said to the lawyer, "I'd like to hear what he has to say about his favorite mule Bessie."

Farmer Joe thanked the judge and proceeded. "Well, as I was saying, I had just loaded Bessie, my favorite mule, into the trailer with a couple of pigs. And I was driving down the highway when this huge semi-truck and trailer ran the stop sign and smacked my truck right in the side. I was thrown into one ditch, and Bessie and the pigs were thrown into the other. I was hurting real bad and didn't want to move. However, I could hear ol' Bessie moaning and groaning. I could hear the pigs squealing. I knew they were in terrible shape just by the noises they were making.

"Shortly after the accident a highway patrolman came on the scene. He could hear Bessie moaning and groaning so he went over to her. After he looked at her, he took out his gun and shot her between the eyes. Then he looked at one of the pigs and shot him. Then he looked at another pig and shot him. Then the patrolman came across the road with his gun in his hand and looked at me. And he said, 'Your mule and a couple of your pigs were in such bad shape I had to shoot them. Now, how are you feeling?' It was then that I said, 'I'm fine.'"

When people are hurting, we don't need to judge them. We need to hear their story. We need to find ways to get them to talk to us about what happened. Let them vent. Let them express themselves. Let them tell their story.

When people are hurting, don't judge them. This is what Job's friends did to him. When they heard what had happened to Job, they went to his home to comfort him. But when they got there and saw all the things that had happened to Job, they all said that Job was being punished because he had sinned. That wasn't for them to say. They didn't know that. When people are hurting, don't judge them. This is what you don't do: Don't make matters worse, and don't judge people who are hurting. Now, let me tell you what you should do.

## A PROCESS

Job 23:10 says, "But he knows the way that I take; when he has tested me, I shall come forth like gold." (NRSV) Job says, things are tough right now but they're going to get better. God knows me. He's knows what is going down. He sees. Things are going to turn around.

See your hurts as a process, not an unmoving event. As someone said the hurt has not happened; it is happening. What do I mean? I mean your painful situation is changing every moment, every hour, every day. It is unfolding. Hurts and afflictions are like everything else in life: they move, they change—they don't stay the same. And as they change you change. Change what? The way you look at it; the way you respond to it.

When you were first hurt, whether it was a friend, a husband, a wife, a child, you probably thought that was the end of the world. But don't look at it like that now. See it as a changing event, a progressing moment in time, turning another chapter of your life, a mountain that, as Jesus said, will be moved if you have faith.

What am I saying? You have to believe that your perception of the hurt is in a process that is moving. It is not immobile; it is not stationary; it is not at rest. It is moving, and if you believe, eventually it will dissipate.

## FACING THE TRUTH

Consider the story of William "the Refrigerator" Perry. Perry was a colorful defensive lineman for the Chicago Bears when they won the Super Bowl back in 1985. His nickname fit him well because he was big and wide. Perry was also a friendly man with a wide grin.

Unfortunately for his grin, though he was a mammoth man playing in the tough world of the football trenches, he apparently was afraid of the dentist, just like most of us. He was so afraid that he didn't go to the dentist for twenty years!

Let's be clear: Some fear is good. God has given us the fear emotion so that our body will spring to action, the fight-or-flight response. When we are afraid, adrenalin kicks in and we are ready, we are alert, we are focused.

As we grow up we must learn about a healthy fear of fire, electricity, and other things that are dangerous. So not all fear is bad.

On the other hand some fear is unhealthy. It will incapacitate you from doing what is right. It paralyzes us from doing things in life. It makes us tentative, unsure, and hesitant. This is the kind of fear from which we need to be set free.

William "the Refrigerator" Perry was afraid of the dentist. He was so afraid that he didn't go to the dentist for twenty years. He didn't go to the dentist even though his teeth and gums hurt terribly, even though his teeth began falling out. Eventually he lost half his teeth—some he pulled out himself!—and his gums suffered chronic infection. He was suffering!

Finally, as he neared age forty-five, he went to a dentist. The dentist had to pull out all of his remaining teeth. He had to insert screws in Perry's jaw and implant new teeth—all of which would have cost Perry $60,000 except the dentist donated the procedure (apparently for the free publicity).

Now there's a story every mother will tell her son when she says he has to go to the dentist or brush his teeth. But this is also a story for all who avoid emotional and spiritual pain of any sort, for the body teaches you things about your soul.

What do I mean? Lots of things that cause pain to the soul actually bring spiritual health—things like asking for help, hard work, repentance, looking honestly into our own souls, going to church, dealing with our problems, humbling ourselves, reading the Bible, listening to sermons, facing the truth. This list goes on.

It takes courage to face pain. But as William Perry said of his new teeth, "It's unbelievable. And I love them....I got tired of my mouth hurting all the time." (Craig Brian Larson, editor of PreachingToday. com; source: "A story with some teeth: Fridge gets a new smile," *Chicago Tribune* (12-20-07) section 4, p. 2)

All of us tend to avoid pain. Sometimes, though, avoiding pain can lead to much greater suffering. Maybe you simply need to face the hurts in your life. You see, some people know they are hurting, and believe it or not they know exactly what is hurting them.

But they keep running from it. They keep ignoring it. They keep pretending the hurt is not there. And no matter how much they try to ignore it they know it is there, and everybody that comes in contact with them knows it is there too. They don't mean to hurt other people, but hurt people hurt people. They lash out at other people for no apparent reason. People who haven't dealt with their hurts are really nice people.

Well, what's the problem? The problem is the pain—the hurt in their lives keeps their beautiful, delightful, charming personalities from beaming through. What am I saying? I'm simply saying if you are hurting don't ignore it—don't close your eyes to it—don't try to overlook it. Face it. You say, how do I do that?

Well, one thing you can do is come to grips with it or recognize what is hurting you. And then don't just talk about the hurt. Instead talk about possible solutions to the person, place, or thing that is hurting you. As someone said, "Don't find fault, find remedies." Focus on what to do next. Spend your energies on moving forward toward finding the answer.

## DON'T HURT OTHERS

Let's look again at our Scripture text, Job 23, because there is something else. Verses 13-15 say,

> But he stands alone and who can dissuade him?
> What he desires, that he does.
> For he will complete what he appoints for me;
> and many such things are in his mind.
> Therefore I am terrified at his presence;
> when I consider, I am in dread of him. (NRSV)

After all Job has lost, he says to his friends Elphaz, Bildad, and Zophar—who told Job earlier that his suffering was because of his sin—that God is God and He can do what He pleases, and God will do exactly what He intends to do with him.

Job says the mere thought of God, the all-powerful, makes him tremble with fear. At this point in Job's discourse what do we hear? We hear a voice that talks about the mightiness of God. You would think after all Job lost that he would have a hatred toward God—a contempt, a dislike, a disdain toward God—but I don't hear that.

I don't even hear a disdain and dislike toward his friends, who didn't make Job feel any better with their reason why they thought he had lost everything. I don't heard hatred in this text. I don't hear contempt in this text.

There is a subtle message here: Don't hate those you feel have hurt you. They have bruised you, yes, but don't hate them.

Dale Carnegie says it like this: When we hate those who we feel have hurt us, we give them power over us—power over our sleep, our appetites, our happiness. They would shout with joy if they knew how much they were worrying us. Our hate is not hurting them at all, but it is turning our days and nights into hellish turmoil.

Don't hate those you feel have hurt you because it is going to ruin you not them—it is going to set you back not them, it's going to mess you up not them, it's going to destroy you not them.

Job says, this thing that has happened to me is tragedy—it is painful and it hurts. But God knows what I'm doing. He knows my life. He knows I haven't always been perfect—no one has—but I have done my best to be faithful, and "when he has tested me I will come forth like pure gold." Notice Job doesn't say he will come out like silver or iron or copper. He says gold, which represents the best out of the situation.

I heard a story recently about a Jewish woman who survived one of the German concentration camps. She endured terrible suffering. She saw lots of people die. And she had to walk miles and miles in the snow without a decent pair of shoes. Sometimes we forget the small things. If you have shoes on your feet, you are blessed. If you have clothes on your back, you are blessed. Many of us complain too much, and we have so much. We forget how much God has blessed us.

At the end of the war the Americans came in and liberated the camp. One of the soldiers told her that he was rescuing her and that she should gather up her things. As she turned to go back to her barracks, the soldier opened the door and held it for her. She started to cry.

The guy said, "What's the matter?"

And the woman replied, "I can't remember the last time someone held a door open for me. It's the nicest thing anyone's done for me in a long time." These two people became friends. They ended up falling in love. And they got married.

Remember that God is like that. He can take our hurts—the bruises—the must horrible situations and make something beautiful come out of it. If you are hurting today, God is saying turn your hurts over to Him and He will make a miracle out of a mess.

- Turn your hurts over to Him because He is the One who can lift burdens.
- Turn your hurts over to Him because He is the One who can renew your joy.
- Turn your hurts over to Him because He is the One who can disburse your fears.

- Turn your hurts over to Him because He is the One who can change your life.
- Turn your hurts over to Him because He is the One — there is no other who can do what He can do.

There is no other who can remove your obstacles. There is no other like Him who can refresh your soul. You may be hurting but remember you have a friend, and His name is Jesus.

- He will listen to you at anytime.
- He will go with you anywhere.
- He will meet you at anyplace.
- He will help you in any situation.
- He will instruct you in any circumstance.
- He will see you through any trial.

You have a friend who knows you, who feels you, who loves you. He knows what you don't know. He can do what you can't do.

- When you are lonely, He will comfort you.
- When you are weak, He will strengthen you.
- When you are anxious, He will assure you
- When you are hurting, He will heal you.

You have a friend who is bigger than your hurts. You have a friend who can transform sorrow and sadness into joy and gladness. You have a friend who can take that which is broken and bruised and battered and bleeding and transform it into a thing of rare beauty. You have a friend who can make a miracle out of a mess.

# CHAPTER THREE

# HOW TO BE HAPPY

**PURPOSE:** To teach and move the hearers to understand that God wants us to be free from our fears.

**READ THE SCRIPTURE:** Matthew 14:22-33

Immediately he made the disciples get into the boat and go on ahead to the other side, while he dismissed the crowds. And after he had dismissed the crowds, he went up the mountain by himself to pray. When evening came, he was there alone, but by this time the boat, battered by the waves, was far from the land, for the wind was against them. And early in the morning he came walking towards them on the lake. But when the disciples saw him walking on the lake, they were terrified, saying, "It is a ghost!" And they cried out in fear. But immediately Jesus spoke to them and said, "Take heart, it is I; do not be afraid." Peter answered him, "Lord, if it is you, command me to come to you on the water." He said, "Come." So Peter got out of the boat, started walking on the water, and came towards Jesus. But when he noticed the strong wind, he became frightened, and beginning to sink, he cried out, "Lord, save me!" Jesus immediately reached out his hand and caught him, saying to him, "You of little faith, why did you doubt?" When they got into the boat, the wind ceased. And those in the boat worshipped him, saying, "Truly you are the Son of God." (NRSV)

Have you ever seen a Dracula movie? When I was a teenager, one of my friends' mothers took us to a Dracula movie. I will never forget that movie. My friend won't either. In fact, I don't let him forget even to this very day. Why? We often joked about it with his mother whenever I was at his house. Although to me it was not a scary movie, my friend was so scared he was afraid to sleep in his room because he always thought that Dracula was in the closet.

He used to ask his older brother to go into the closet and see if Dracula was in there. And his older brother would go in the closet and come out and pronounce with his mouth wide open and ketchup dripping from his tongue, "Yes, Dracula is in there, and I'm sure glad I don't have to sleep in this room!"

Fear starts early in life. Someone tells us a scary story when we are young. We see a scary movie or a scary picture, and sometimes that scary picture or horror flick never leaves us. Someone profoundly said our childhood is what we spend the rest of our lives overcoming.

Fear starts early in life. Our fear might have started when we were young, but fears are all around us right now: global warming, loss of jobs, swine flu, terrorist plots, North Korean nuclear bombs getting in the hands of the wrong people, Iraq and the Afghanistan War, and Iran's relentless pursuit of nuclear weapons.

## PERSONAL FEARS

But most of the fears we carry around with us aren't these big societal fears. Instead they are the personal fears. What are some of the personal fears that we carry around? Some of us are afraid of failure. I remember when I was fifteen years old and played baseball. This particular year we made it to the championship game. There were two outs, two people on base, and it was my turn to hit—and I was not a great hitter. In fact, I was one of the worst hitters on the team. I thought, "Why me? Why is it my turn to hit?"

My coach called me over and said, "Son, don't swing. Wait for a walk." I said to myself, "Don't swing. I can do that." Well, I strolled to the plate, trembling and sweating profusely. I put my bat up on my shoulder, looked at the pitcher as he looked at me (I swear he could see right through me), and I felt like I was in a tunnel and it was just him and me.

As he got ready to pitch the ball, he lifted his leg, drew the ball into his mitt, kicked out his leg, and threw the ball. Why did I do it? I don't understand why. But I did the opposite of what my coach told me to do. I swung at the ball. And to make matters worse it was nowhere in the strike zone. In fact, it was above my head. You are not going to believe this, but he threw two balls above my head and I swung at both of them. But I finally got smart. The next two balls I didn't swing at and both were balls.

So I had a full house—two strikes and two balls. I stepped back from the plate then stepped back up to the plate, determined not to swing. I want you to know I didn't swing—that's right, I didn't swing. But you know what? The pitcher threw the ball in the strike zone, and of course the umpire called a strike and there began one of the worst times in my life. I felt I caused us to lose the championship game. The next year I decided not to play. When the season started my coach called my house and asked me where I was, and I said I was never going to play baseball again.

Some of us are afraid of failure. We fear not meeting the mark or goal that we set or others have set for us. Disappointing ourselves and people we care about—mother, father, sisters, brothers, associates—can keep us from taking on a task, from dreaming, and from trying again when we have failed. Some of us have financial fears, finding it hard to make ends meet, so we fear that we may lose our house or car or job.

Some people are afraid that others might not like them. When you think everybody has to like you that is a sign of low self-esteem. There are times when we need to be humble, but there are also times when we need to think good and beautiful thoughts about ourselves.

One day a man went to an auction. While there, he bid on an exotic parrot. He really wanted this bird, so he got caught up in the bidding. He kept on bidding but kept getting outbid, so he bid higher and higher and higher. Finally, after he bid way more than he intended, he won the bid. The price was high but the fine bird was finally his.

As he was paying for the parrot, he said to the auctioneer, "I sure hope this parrot can talk. I would hate to have paid this much for it only to find out he can't talk!"

"Don't worry," said the auctioneer. "He can talk. Who do you think kept bidding against you?"

Some people are afraid that others might not like them. But to conquer that fear, you have to start thinking highly of yourself. Because if you don't think you are worth anything, nobody else will.

## HEALTHY FEAR AND BAD FEAR

Too many of us are filled with fears—fear of speaking in public, fear of tight places, fear of being alone, fear of losing control, fear of loud noises, fear of rejection, fear of our past. The list goes on.

I remember when I was a child around eight or nine years old, and we were outside playing with firecrackers. I never really liked firecrackers although I liked throwing grenades when I was in the Marine Corps. One day when I was a kid a friend put a firecracker in my hand and said, "Now I'm going to light it and then you throw it." After he lit it, I just stood there with the firecracker in my hand. I finally decided to throw it but it was too late; the firecracker almost blew my fingers off.

As we said earlier, some fear is good. It protects us. But there are some today who seek to live with "no fear." Their approach is to adopt a feeling of recklessness and apathy. These people say things like "whatever" all the time. They have no fear because they just don't care. Living with "no fear" in this way is not positive but is actually irresponsible, reckless, and detrimental. These people would profit from a little healthy fear. So there is healthy fear and bad fear. In this chapter, I am talking about the bad fear. Why? Because too many of us are filled with it, and we need to be free from it.

In Matthew 14:27 it says, But immediately Jesus spoke to them and said, "Take heart, it is I; do not be afraid." (NRSV) Jesus and the disciples had spent the day with some 5,000 people. Jesus taught them and then he miraculously fed them all with just a bit of bread and fish. After Jesus taught all those people, he put his disciples into a boat and had them set sail for the other side of the Sea of Galilee. Meanwhile, Jesus went off by himself to pray. The disciples were in the boat, far away from land when a great storm swept down on them. The disciples strained against the oars. The wind was fierce and they were fighting heavy waves. To their utter consternation, they saw what appeared to be a ghost come toward them and they cried out in terror. But it was Jesus! "It's all right," he said, "I am here! Don't be afraid."

For a total of 366 times in the Bible God tells us to "fear not." Let me tell you what that says to me. It says to me that God wants us to be free from fears that hinder our spiritual growth. God doesn't want us walking around panicky about everything. Why? Matthew 14:28 gives a clue: "Peter, suddenly, bold, said, "Master, if it is really you, call me to come to you on the water." (Message) Some people say

Peter was putting Jesus to a test here in this verse. I don't believe so. I believe he was the only one in the boat acting in faith.

God wants us to be free from fears that hinder our spiritual growth because He wants us to respond to whatever circumstances we encounter, to whatever trials we face, with faith not doubt. Not with misgivings but with faith. And we can't do that when we are full of fear. But so many people have a problem reacting with faith because they are so filled with fear. And that is not how God wants us to be. How do we get free from our fears?

## RELEASE

Matthew 14:28 says: "Peter answered, 'If it is you, command me to come to you on the water.'" To get free from fear, take those things in your life that you cannot change and mentally put them— which includes yourself—in God's hands. God wants to give you peace, and He will give you peace. In John 14:26-27, the Lord says: "Don't be upset...trust God...trust Me! I am leaving you with a gift—peace of mind and heart. And the peace I give, the world isn't giving it to you and the world can't take it away. So, don't be troubled or afraid!"

I heard a story about a train traveling through the night in a violent rainstorm. The lightning flashes were almost blinding, the rain hitting the windows was deafening, and the strong gusts of wind rocked the train from side to side. When the lightning flashed and lit up the darkness, the passengers could see the rising water along the tracks. This created terror in the minds of the passengers. Several passengers noted that through all the noise, lightning, and wind, one of the passengers, a little girl, seemed to be at perfect peace. The adult passengers couldn't figure out why the little girl was so calm during all this excitement.

Finally, one passenger asked her, "How is it that you can be so calm when all the rest of us are so worried about what might happen?" The little passenger smiled and said, "My father is the engineer."

Those things you cannot change—and there may be some in your life right now—you must release to God, because God wants to give you peace, not just peace for the moment (and that may be all you're concerned about right now), but also peace in any situation. No matter how brutal and bumpy the storm, God can give you peace. No matter how tough the storm, God can give you peace.

A television program preceding the 1988 Winter Olympics featured blind skiers being trained for slalom skiing, impossible as that sounds. Paired with sighted skiers, the blind skiers were taught on the flats how to make right and left turns. When that was mastered, they were taken to the slalom slope, where their sighted partners skied beside them shouting "Left!" and "Right!" (Robert Sutton)

As they obeyed the commands, they were able to negotiate the course and cross the finish line, depending solely on the sighted skiers' word. It was either complete trust or catastrophe. What a vivid picture of the Christian life! In this world, we are in reality blind about what course to take. We must rely solely on the Word of the only One who is truly sighted—God Himself. His Word gives us the direction we need to finish the course.

As you navigate the slippery slopes of life, God will direct you. He'll tell you when to turn right; He'll tell you when to turn left. He'll help you conquer your fears and get to the finish line of life. Take those events in your life (spiritual, emotional, physical) that you cannot change, you have to put them in God's hands, and He will negotiate you through the course of life.

## MEMORIZE

To free yourself from fear, not only should you take those things in your life that you cannot change and mentally put them in God's hands, but you should also memorize biblical promises. There are some promises in the Bible that we need to memorize. Sometimes you just can't get to your Bible so you need to memorize some of the verses. Let's look at a few of those biblical promises. Psalm 23 says:

> The Lord is my shepherd, I shall not want.
> He makes me lie down in green pastures;
> he leads me beside still waters;
> he restores my soul.
> He leads me in right paths
> for his name's sake.
> Even though I walk through the darkest valley,
> I fear no evil;
> for you are with me;
> your rod and your staff—

they comfort me.
You prepare a table before me
in the presence of my enemies;
you anoint my head with oil;
my cup overflows.
Surely goodness and mercy shall follow me
all the days of my life,
and I shall dwell in the house of the LORD
my whole life long. (NRSV)

Isaiah 43 says:

But now thus says the LORD,
he who created you, O Jacob,
he who formed you, O Israel:
Do not fear, for I have redeemed you;
I have called you by name, you are mine.
When you pass through the waters, I will be with you;
and through the rivers, they shall not overwhelm you;
when you walk through fire you shall not be burned,
and the flame shall not consume you. (NRSV)

To free yourself from your fears, memorize biblical promises such as Psalm 23: "Even though I walk through the darkest valley, I will fear no evil...for you are with me." Memorize Isaiah 43:5: "Fear not! For I am with you." These are just two of the multitude of biblical promises you can memorize to help you cope with fear. The Bible is full of them.

At a fair one day, people were selling various wares. Among them was a woman selling medicine and a man selling Bibles. Some wicked young men came to the woman and jestingly said, "Do you think your medicine will cure us?"

To this she replied, "What is the matter with you?"

They sarcastically replied, "Oh, we have the devil in us."

The woman replied, "No, my medicine will not cure you." Then, pointing to the man selling Bibles, she said, "He has the medicine that you need, and it will cure you. (William Moses Tidwell, (Pointed Illustrations [elbourne.org])

I don't know what you are dealing with, what fear has you entangled, but I am sure that memorizing some Bible verses will help. It has the medicine that can cure any fear—any anxiety, any demon spirit—you may have.

## ACCOMPANIED

Not only should you memorize biblical promises to help free yourself of unhealthy fears, but also remember the key to handling fearful times is knowing that you are not facing them alone—God is on your side.

If it were up to us, we would have God help us by taking us away from what terrifies us. Isn't that what we would ask God to do? "God, I'm afraid of this. Please take it away. Please remove it from my presence." But God will not give us a pass so that we don't have to deal with fear.

God promises something else instead. Read and listen to part of Psalm 23, specifically verse 4 again: "Yea though I walk through the valley of the shadow of death, I will fear no evil; for thou art with me." Underline the word "through" in that verse.

In Isaiah 43:1-2, we hear the Word of the Lord saying (as you read this underline the word "through" every time it appears in this text):

> But now thus says the Lord,
> He who created you, Jacob,
> He who formed you, O Israel:
> Do not fear, for I have redeemed you;
> I have called you by name, you are mine.
> When you pass through the waters, I will be with you;
> And through the rivers, they shall not overwhelm you;
> When you walk through fire you shall not be burned,
> And the flame shall not consume you. (NRSV)

Note that the operative word in both passages is "through" not "stay in." When God tells us to fear not, it is not "Fear not, for I'll take you out of the situation"; instead it is, "Fear not, I'll be with you in the situation." That is what gives us the audacity and guts to face our fears. God being on your side means that He will see you through. God being on your side means you cannot lose. Isn't that what you want? You can have it, but you have to remember that whatever you are facing you are not facing it alone.

## CONVICTIONS

In addition to knowing that you are not facing your fears alone, your convictions should be to trust God rather than your fears. Ralph

Waldo Emerson said, "Fear defeats more people than any one thing in the world." In Matthew 4:27-29, we hear these words:

> But immediately Jesus spoke to them and said, "Take heart, it is I; do not be afraid." Peter answered him, "Lord, if it is you, command me to come to you on the water." He said, "Come." So Peter got out of the boat, started walking on the water, and came towards Jesus. (NRSV)

Peter was not the only one in that boat. There were other disciples with him, but in that storm, as the waves and wind buffeted against the boat, every one of them except Peter was terrified. In the storm, their reaction was one of fear and not faith — but not Peter. He decided to trust the Lord rather than fear.

Do you want freedom from the unhealthy fears that are destroying your life? Do you want freedom from unwholesome fears that are freezing your faith? Then do what Peter did when he saw Jesus out walking on the water: Trust God rather than fear.

Every time I have trusted God rather than fear I have grown in my relationship with God. Something important happens each time I face my fears. And so God told me to tell you, each time you face a scary challenge, each time you are fearful and you face it, each time you face it head-on, you will get a little stronger inside. You will build up the core of who you are, and you will begin to trust God more than you did before.

Each time you refuse to take the difficult step, each time you turn back, each time you allow your fears to convince you that your fears are bigger than God, your faith diminishes.

That's why it is so important to face our fears with God leading us. When we face our fears with God leading us, we conquer those fears. When we decide to stay faithful in a situation that we do not like and cannot understand, when we keep walking even though we see the strong whistling wind, when we keep walking even though we see the storm, when we keep walking even though we see the lightning flashing trying to conquer our soul, we discover that somehow we are not alone; we discover that the Lord is with us; we discover that the Lord is a very present help in a time of need, and we grow a bit braver and a bit stronger each time.

I don't know what fear is raging like a storm under your feet. It could be a character flaw you fear you might never overcome, it could be someone you love who has not come to Christ, it could be debt and financial pressure, it could be anxiety, or it could be something else (only you and God know). But God's message to you is don't look down at it. Keep your eyes on Jesus, and He will get you through it.

Peter started out right. He acted out of faith rather than fear. But when things got a little rough as he walked on the water he took his eyes off the One who helped him to make it in the first place.

- No matter how rough it gets, keep your eyes on Jesus.

- No matter how dark it gets, keep your eyes on Jesus.
- No matter how bumpy it gets, keep your eyes on Jesus.

Trust the Lord rather than fear. Don't react in fear and turn to cultic methods and practices to get you out of your dilemma.

- Don't respond in fear and rely upon schemes and ingenuity to help you overcome your adversity.
- Don't respond in fear and assume that everything will work out on its own.

Trust in the Lord rather than fear. Put your trust and confidence in God rather than fear. Keep your eyes on Jesus.

- Believe when others doubt.
- Go forth when others hold back.
- Work when others sleep.
- Stand when others flee.

Keep your eyes on Jesus because He will help you bear your burdens. He will help you to dispel your fears.

- He will help you to carry your load.
- He will help you to handle your problems.
- He will help you to survive your crises.

- He will help you to stand your ground.
- He will help you to win your victory.

# CHAPTER FOUR

# FEELING GOOD ABOUT LIFE

**PURPOSE:** To teach you to understand that God wants you to feel good about life

**READ THE SCRIPTURE:** Philippians 4:10-15

I rejoice in the Lord greatly that now at last you have revived your concern for me; indeed, you were concerned for me, but had no opportunity to show it. Not that I am referring to being in need; for I have learned to be content with whatever I have. I know what it is to have little, and I know what it is to have plenty. In any and all circumstances I have learned the secret of being well-fed and of going hungry, of having plenty and of being in need. I can do all things through him who strengthens me. In any case, it was kind of you to share my distress. (NRSV)

I read this poem the other day, and it really caught my attention. I said to myself, who would write such a poem? What is wrong with this person? The poem went like this:

Life is never good for me and this is what I wish you'd see. Just let me end it all for I'll be happy in the end, I'll finally be free.

Free from all the pain and torment and the never ending battle. No more dealing with the arguments and tears, I'd finally be through with it all.

You just don't seem to understand that by keeping me here your [sic] making it worse. If I were dead and gone by now I'd be happy, I wouldn't have this life, I wouldn't have the curse.

I'm already considering doing this even without your consent. I know for sure that once its [sic] all over with my heart will finally be content. So here I am just sitting there, on my bed with a knife to my wrist.

Please everyone don't be upset, please don't be pissed. You just need to know I love you all but couldn't handle it anymore. Ok here I go, I'm doing this for sure.

You just need to let me go to heaven now, hopefully God will understand and accept this. Just tell my baby I love him and I'm sorry I couldn't give him one last kiss.

Tell everyone I love them and that I'm sorry I had to go so soon and leave them all behind. But I just needed to end it all and start a new life so happiness I could find. These are the last words I'll ever be writing down.

I know they are harsh but don't worry, rest your head, be at ease, don't make a sound. Know that I love you and always have but I need to think of me right now and so I said goodbye.

Be happy without me and know that I'm somewhere good, somewhere up high. I just hope your [sic] not crying, I want you to know everything will be ok. I'll be watching over you and listening to what you have to say.

Just have patience, wait till the day, and I'll see you up here in heaven and we can be together. Except this time things will be better and you'll see me happy, always and forever. So stop your weeping and know this was the best thing for me.

It was my time to go, your time to set me free.

(Manda Prosser, Buzzleme.com)

There are just too many people who do not feel good about life. They wake up depressed. They go to work depressed. They come home depressed. They try to go to church, and they still don't feel any better about life. Why?

## STUFF WILL SATISFY

Ecclesiastes 5:10 says: "The lover of money will not be satisfied with money; nor the lover of wealth, with gain. This is vanity." (NRSV)

Solomon says the one who loves money is never satisfied with money, nor the one who loves wealth with big profits. It is nothing but smoke and will soon vanish.

Let's look at it this way. How would you complete this sentence: "I think I could finally be satisfied if _____." Or how about this sentence: "I would feel quite happy in life if _____." Don't just write something down. Think about this question for a few minutes and be honest with yourself. Most people, if they are truly honest with themselves, would fill in that blank with some kind of material thing.

- If I had more money
- If I had a brand-new sports car or Cadillac
- If I had the job I want
- If I could marry the person of my dreams
- If I could build my dream house

- If I could get a certain promotion or position
- If I could gain a certain position of influence
- If I could solve a certain problem
- If I didn't have to do something

We would pin our hope to some of the very things Solomon says are meaningless. Solomon had money, pleasure, knowledge, beautiful women, and status, and they left him unsatisfied. The problem is that we don't believe him. We think it would be different for us. We wouldn't be miserable. We would be happy.

Do you think most people in Hollywood are content? Look at professional athletes. They have everything (materially) that anyone could want, but do they look content? Some are strung out on drugs, alcohol, extramarital sex. What am I saying to you? I am saying that the inescapable conclusion is that having stuff isn't what makes you happy or brings you satisfaction. Some people do not feel good about life because they believe that stuff will satisfy them. No matter how much you earn, if you try to create happiness by accumulating wealth, you will never have enough.

## RESPONSIBLE

Matthew 27:24 says: "So when Pilate saw that he could do nothing, but rather that a riot was beginning, he took some waters and washed his hands before the crowd saying, 'I am innocent of this man's blood; see to it yourselves.'" (NRSV)

The religious leaders had accused Jesus of various crimes, and they wanted Pilate to make a ruling on it. Pilate didn't even want to make a decision as to whether Jesus would be released from His accusers. So what does Pilate do? He makes no decision at all.

A little girl had been trying for months to learn the art of tying her shoes. She finally grasped the knack and was able to do it by herself. Her parents expected her to be delighted, and they were surprised by her disappointment. Her father asked why she was crying.

She sobbed, "I just learned how to tie my shoes."

He said, "That's wonderful, honey, but why are you crying?"

She replied, "Because now I'll have to do it all by myself for the rest of my life." (The Sermon on the Amount," Heidi Husted, Preaching Today, Tape 122.)

Some people don't feel good about life because they don't like the responsibility that comes with it. All of us have to deal with life, but some people don't want any responsibility. Some people never want to grow up. They don't want to have to make any decisions.

Philippians 4:8 says: "Finally, beloved, whatever is true, whatever is honourable, whatever is just, whatever is pure, whatever is pleasing, whatever is commendable, if there is any excellence and if there is anything worthy of praise, think about these things." (NRSV)

What is God saying here? He is saying that we should fill our minds with the best not the worst—the beautiful not the ugly—things to praise not things to curse. He is talking about things that draw a beautiful, lovely picture about life, things that make us feel good.

A speaker in Colorado was about to address a gathering of businessmen and women. Sitting at the head table, he turned to the real estate salesman on his left and said, "So how are things going for you?"

"Terrible," the salesman answered. "Haven't you heard about the strikes? Eight percent of the people in this town are employed by just two firms, and they are both on strike! Business is horrible. I haven't sold a piece of property since the strike. I don't even have any listings. I've had to lay off three salespeople, and if things don't turn around soon I'll go bankrupt."

The speaker turned to the saleswoman on his right and asked the same question. She said, "Haven't you heard about the strike?"

"Yes," he answered.

Then she went on. "Business couldn't be better. Since the strike I've sold more houses than ever. And if the strike continues for a while, I'll be rich!"

"How's that?" the speaker asked.

"Well, you see, I figured that since the folks were on strike, they would have lots of time to search for their dream house. And I reasoned with them that when the strike is settled, they're going to get a nice raise. Enough to purchase the house they've always wanted."

God is very optimistic with regard to the human race. After all, He invested His life for us. We ought to imitate Him. God wants us to feel good about life. He doesn't want us depressed. He doesn't want us thinking about how life is going to defeat us. He wants us to be optimistic, upbeat, cheerful, positive. That's why throughout His ministry on earth Jesus talked about abundant life—forgiveness and grace and mercy.

He doesn't want us to feel down, but up; not depressed, but happy; not miserable, but content. He wants us to feel good about life. What is it that we need to do to feel good about life?

## MINDSET

Let's look at Philippians 4 because it holds some answers to our question. In verses 12-13 we read: "I know what it is to have little, and I know what it is to have plenty. In any and all circumstances I have learned the secret of being well-fed and of going hungry, of having plenty and of being in need. I can do all things through him who strengthens me." (NRSV)

When Paul wrote this he was in a Roman prison. Paul says, "I've learned by now to be quite content whatever my circumstances. I'm just as happy with little as with much, with much as with little. I've found the recipe for being happy whether full or hungry, hands full or hands empty. Whatever I have, wherever I am, I can make it through anything in the One who makes me who I am. I don't mean that your help didn't mean a lot to me—it did. It was a beautiful thing that you came alongside me in my troubles."

Although Paul was in a prison do you notice his attitude? Do you notice his approach to his situation? Do you notice (it is not hard to see) his outlook, his posture, his feelings despite his predicament?

There is a story about an eighty-four-year-old grandmother who fiercely maintained her independence and lived alone in the old family home. Her four children lived in the same town, but she rarely called them except in emergencies.

It was with some apprehension therefore that one of her sons drove to her house one morning in answer to her phone call. When he arrived she said she suspected there was a burglar in her bedroom closet, since she had heard noises in there the night before.

"Why didn't you call me last night?" he exclaimed.

"Well," she replied, "it was late and I hated to bother you, so I just nailed the closet shut and went to bed."

Feeling good about life is not about circumstance—it is about attitude. The right attitude can take you a long way no matter what condition you are in or what your circumstance may be. The right attitude says "I will trust that God has a reason for the things that are going on in my life. He has a plan to use me and develop me through these things."

## THE BLESSINGS

In Philippians 12:4 we hear these words: "I know what it is to have little, and I know what it is to have plenty." Paul says to the church "whatever I have at any given moment in life, I enjoy that."

Two men were walking along and one of them was rubbing on a stone he took out of his pocket. The other man said, "What's that you have in your hand?"

The other man replied, "It's my grateful stone. Every time I think about what I don't have or something in the past that depresses me, I rub this stone to remind me to remember what good times I have in my life right now. I take this stone with me everywhere I go."

To feel good about life we need to enjoy the blessings we have now. Quit worrying about what you don't have and look at what you do have. Enjoy the blessings you have today: family, job, house, health, joy. How exactly do you do this? Enjoy the blessings you have now.

Native hunters in the jungles of Africa have a clever way of trapping monkeys. They slice a coconut in two, hollow it out, and in one half of the shell they cut a hole just big enough for a monkey's hand to pass through.

Then they place an orange in the other coconut half before fastening together the two halves of the coconut shell. Finally, they secure the coconut to a tree with a rope, retreat into the jungle, and wait. Sooner or later an unsuspecting monkey swings by, smells the delicious orange, and discovers its location inside the coconut.

The monkey slips his hand through the small hole, grasps the orange, and tries to pull it through the hole. Of course, the orange won't come out; it's too big for the hole. To no avail the persistent monkey continues to pull and pull, never realizing the danger he is in.

While the monkey struggles with the orange, the hunters simply stroll in and capture the monkey by throwing a net over him. As long as the monkey keeps his fist wrapped around the orange, he is trapped. It's too bad—the poor monkey could save his own life if he would let go of the orange. It rarely occurs to a monkey, however, that it can't have both the orange and its freedom. That delicious orange becomes a deadly trap.

To enjoy the blessings you have now, don't live in the past. Let go of things that are draining you. There is nothing you can do to change or correct the past—that can only be done in the present. Today, change what you need to change; let go of those things that have you trapped—fear, hate, doubt, disappointment—and move on to feel good about your life.

And then don't waste your time on what you can't control, like people. Concentrate on what you can control. What do I mean? I mean you can control who you hug, what you read, when you smile, how much you laugh, where you go, what you do, what you think about. Don't waste your time, your energy, your resources on what you can't control.

And then write down everything you are grateful for now. Write down everything in your life that you have now that makes you happy. The result will be a recognition that you have more to be thankful for than you first realized; more to be upbeat about than you first realized; more to look forward to than you first realized; more blessings emerging in your life than you ever realized.

## ASSESSMENT

In Philippians 4:12b, Paul says: "In any and all circumstances I have learned the secret of being well-fed and going hungry, of having plenty and being in need." (NRSV)

Paul had a healthy self-image. He felt good about himself being able to handle whatever came his way.

James Moore, a minister and author of many books, tells the story about a lady who came to him a couple of years ago and wanted him to arrange for her to see a psychiatrist. She was seeking help. I don't know exactly what your problem is, but someone who is reading this book needs help, and I hear God saying "are you willing to let Me help you?" When we face difficult or frightening situations, we must be willing to let God help.

This woman who came to Pastor Moore was seeking help. The woman said she had a problem that was getting out of hand. "I'm extremely jealous and I resent the good fortune of my friends, and I am so suspicious of my husband that I'm afraid I may fly into a rage and cause someone to get hurt," she told Pastor Moore.

So Pastor Moore said he referred her to a psychiatrist. After one session the psychiatrist called him and said, "I know her problem. She doesn't like herself, and she can't like or love anyone else until she learns how to feel good about herself."

Self-hate is dangerous. It can lead to volatile jealousy and cause us to hurt other people, even those closest to us. To feel good about life, you have to like yourself. You have to have a healthy self-image. Some people don't feel good about life because they don't have a healthy self-image.

Rodney Dangerfield said he was so ugly when he was born the doctor slapped his mama. He said he was so unlucky when he was a child that his rocking horse died.

To feel good about life you have to like yourself. You need to have a strong sense of self and a positive self-esteem. Suppose you don't have it and you want to have it, what can you do? I think one of the things you can do is look in the mirror and instead of saying "I look terrible in this shirt," say "I look really nice in this shirt." Or "I look good in this dress." Or just simply say to yourself, "I like me. I love me." Be confident—not arrogant, but confident—in the way you look; self-confidence never hurt anybody. It will improve your self-image and thereby help you to feel good about life. It's hard to feel good about life when you don't like yourself. You can have all the money in the world, all the friends in the world, all the talent in the world—sing, dance, travel, dress well, communicate, write—but it's hard to be happy when you don't like *you*.

## MORE OF GOD

In Philippians 4:13 we read these words: "I can do all things through him who strengthens me." (NRSV) Notice the phrase "I can do all things." You know, Paul had a tremendous amount of faith in God. Paul says "I can do all things through God"—not some things, not a few things, but all things. Paul says "whatever I have, wherever I am, I can make it through anything in the One who makes me who I am."

Bill and Gloria Gaither have written many wonderful Christian songs. One that Gloria wrote in the late 1960s came while she was expecting a child. The couple was going through some terrible problems. Bill had been seriously sick and their music had been attacked as not spiritual.

On New Year's Eve, Gloria sat in a dark room experiencing a time of torment and fear. She said, "I sat alone in the darkness thinking about the rebellious world and all of our problems—and about our baby yet unborn. Who in their right mind would bring a child into a world like this?" She was at the height of her fear, and then something happened.

She said, "I can't quite explain what happened in that next moment, but suddenly I felt released from it all. The panic that had begun to build inside was gently dispelled by a reassuring presence and a soft voice that kept saying, 'Don't forget the empty tomb, don't forget the empty tomb.' Then I knew I could have that baby and face the future with optimism and trust for I had been reminded that it was all worth it just because He lives."

That night she wrote: "How sweet to hold a newborn baby, and feel the pride and joy he gives; but greater still the calm assurance, this child can face uncertain days because He lives. Because He lives I can face tomorrow, because He lives all fear is gone, because I know He holds the future. And life is worth the living just because He lives."

Not only must you have the right attitude, not only must you enjoy your present blessings, not only must you like yourself, but to feel good about life you also have to trust God more. You have to know that whatever the future holds, you and God can successfully tackle it together. No, sometimes it will not be easy. Sometimes life will test your faith. But you just have to trust God more.

- Trust God more, and He will help you to live one day at a time.
- Trust God more, and He will help you to lie down and rest at night when you think you can't.
- Trust God more, and He will help you to overcome your disappointments and fears.

You have come this far by faith. You thought you weren't going to make it but you did. And do you know how you got this far? You leaned on the Lord. So lean on Him now.

- Trust in Him now.
- Put your faith in Him now.

- Have confidence in Him now.
- Believe in Him now.

This ain't the only time it's been dark in your life. There were other times. There were other times you didn't feel good about life. But that storm cloud passed over, that difficult time passed over. Not because you were so good, not because you have money in your pocket, not because you have food on your table, but the storm cloud passed over because God was with you. The storm clouds passed over because God promised to be your anchor in the storm. The storm clouds passed over because God promised never, never to leave you alone.

- You can face tomorrow because that same God is still with you right now.
- You can face tomorrow because God is going to supply your needs according to His riches in glory.
- You can face tomorrow because God is going to change your circumstances.
- You can face tomorrow because God has promised to hear you when you pray.
- You can face tomorrow because the Lord is your Shepherd.

o   The Lord is your strength.

o   The Lord is your shield.

o   The Lord is your refuge.

o   The Lord is your blessing.

o   The Lord is your Rock.

o   The Lord is your way maker.

You can face tomorrow and the next day and the next day... because the angels of the Lord are encamped around you.

# CHAPTER FIVE

---

# USING THIS OPPORTUNITY
# TO FORGIVE

**PURPOSE:** To teach and move the hearers to understand that we need to use the opportunity to forgive.

**READ THE SCRIPTURE:** Luke 15:11-24

Then Jesus said, "There was a man who had two sons. The younger of them said to his father, 'Father, give me the share of the property that will belong to me.' So he divided his property between them. A few days later the younger son gathered all he had and travelled to a distant country, and there he squandered his property in dissolute living.

"When he had spent everything, a severe famine took place throughout that country, and he began to be in need. So he went and hired himself out to one of the citizens of that country, who sent him to his fields to feed the pigs. He would gladly have filled himself with the pods that the pigs were eating; and no one gave him anything.

"But when he came to himself he said, 'How many of my father's hired hands have bread enough and to spare, but here I am dying of hunger! I will get up and go to my father, and I will say to him, "Father, I have sinned against heaven and before you; I am no longer worthy to be called your son; treat me like one of your hired hands.'" So he set off and went to his father. But while he was still far off, his father saw him and was filled with compassion; he ran and put his arms around him and kissed him. Then the son said to him, 'Father, I have sinned against heaven and before you; I am no longer worthy to be called your son.'

"But the father said to his slaves, 'Quickly, bring out a robe—the best one—and put it on him; put a ring on his finger and sandals on his feet. And get the fatted calf and kill it, and let us eat and celebrate; for this son of mine was dead and is alive again; he was lost and is found!' And they began to celebrate." (NRSV)

How are you entering each day? What are you carrying in your heart as you enter each brand-new day, each brand-new season? A man said to his son as they were talking, "Son, I never knew what real happiness was until I got married...and then it was too late." How are you entering each brand-new day, each brand-new season? What are you carrying in your heart as you enter this brand-new day?

A grandmother overheard her five-year-old granddaughter playing "wedding." The wedding vows went like this: "You have the right to remain silent, anything you say may be held against you, you have the right to have an attorney present. You may kiss the bride."

How are you entering this season at this time? What are you carrying in your heart as you enter this brand-new hour, this brand-new day, this brand-new week?

Many of us are entering another day, another season, with unforgiveness in our hearts. There is someone who did something to us that we have not forgiven. They bruised us in some way. They insulted us in some way. And we have determined in our hearts that we would never look beyond their heinous act and forgive them.

The Prodigal Son, also known as the Lost Son, is one of the best known parables of Jesus. You can read about this story only in the Gospel of Luke. Jesus illustrates the story of a man who has two sons. The younger frivolous son demands his share of his inheritance while his father is still living and goes off to a distant country where he "waste[s] his substance with riotous living." Eventually he has to take work as a swineherd. This was obviously a low point for the younger son because swine are unclean in Judaism.

There he comes to his senses. He decides to return home and beg for his father's mercy, thinking that even if his father does refuse to acknowledge him, being one of his servants is still far better than feeding pigs. But when he returns home, his father doesn't even give him a chance to beg for mercy. He kills a fatted calf to celebrate his son's return. The older brother is forlorn and gets upset about the favored treatment his faithless brother is receiving and justifiably complains of the lack of reward for his own faithfulness. But the father responds, "My son, you are always with me, and everything I have is yours. But we had to celebrate, be filled with joy, and be glad, because this brother of yours was dead and is alive again; he was lost and is found."

We need to use this opportunity we have during each day, each season, to do what this father did. You say what did he do? He forgave someone who obviously hurt him. We need to use this opportunity today to forgive. Life is fleeting, and we don't have long to make things right. Someone needs your forgiveness, and you know who they are. Someone needs to be pardoned by you for their behavior. You can use this moment, this day, to let them off the hook. I am not saying let them hurt you again. No, I am not saying that. But what I am saying is that you don't need to hold that unforgiveness in your heart any longer. Let me show you why forgiving the person is necessary.

In Luke 15:20 it says, "So he set off and went to his father. But while he was still far off, his father saw him and was filled with compassion; he ran and put his arms around him and kissed him." (NRSV)

This story is symbolic. It is metaphorical. The father is supposed to represent God and the boy is supposed to represent us. The boy in this text had done wrong but his father forgave him. And you know what? That boy needs to always remember that. You see, there is going to come a moment in that boy's life—it might be tomorrow, the next day, or two years or more down the road—that someone is going to hurt him like he hurt his father. And you know what that boy needs to do? He needs to remember what his father did for him when he broke his heart.

Romans 5:8 says, "But God proved his love for us in that while we were still sinners Christ died for us." (NRSV) Underline the phrase "While we were still sinners." These words are amazing. God sent Jesus to die for us, not because we were good enough, but because He loves us.

We need to forgive others who wronged us because God forgave us when we did wrong against Him. We need to forgive. God forgave us. Or have you forgotten? Have you forgotten that when you did wrong God looked beyond your fault and saw your need? Have you forgotten that when you did wrong God looked down from heaven and gave you a second, a third, a fourth, a fifth chance? We deserved hell, punishment, and everything that comes with it, but we escaped it because God forgave us.

Lewis B. Smedes profoundly said, "Forgiveness is God's invention for coming to terms with a world in which, despite their best intentions, people are unfair to each other and hurt each other deeply. He began by forgiving us. And he invites us all to forgive each other."

We need to forgive others who wronged us because God forgave us when we did wrong against Him. And perhaps you are saying as you read this, "But what they did—their act, their behavior (when they wronged me)—was not innocuous, it was not harmless. It bruised me deeply. How do I go about forgiving someone who hurt me?" And that is a good question: How do we forgive someone who hurt us? Let's explore this. Let's delve into this question and see what can be done.

One of the first places I always look for answers when I am troubled is in the Word of God. This is also the case when I am writing a book. The Word of God has every answer to every question we have. Another thing I do is read as many books and articles on the subject I will be teaching as possible. And so as I prepared for this chapter of the book, I read the Bible of course, and then I read books and articles about forgiveness.

I read books like *Is Forgiveness Possible* by John Patton; *The Unburdened Heart: Five Keys to Forgiveness and Freedom* by Mariah Burton Nelson; *From Anger to Forgiveness* by Earnie Larson; *Recovering the Power of Repentance & Forgiveness* by Dr. Leah Coulter; *On Forgiveness* by Richard Holloway; *The Five Steps to Forgiveness: The Art and Science of Forgiving* by Dr. Everett Worthington; and *The Forgiving Self: The Road from Resentment to Connection* by Robert Karen.

After I read the Bible and read these books on the subject, I went back to the Bible with several solutions to forgiving in my mind to see if these solutions are biblical. Why? Sometimes the solution sounds good, but if it is not biblical then it is my belief that it will not work over the long haul. In other words, an unbiblical solution may sound good and start out working—it may appear to be a strong bridge, but eventually it will crumple under the pressure of time.

Biblical solutions are always able to sustain and endure the stress and strain of time. This is why I check book facts against biblical facts. So what I give you in this section of my book was discovered in my probing of other books and articles, and my own experience, but I checked these solutions against the Word of God, as you should always do also.

## AN APOLOGY

Let's take a look at Luke 15:20: "So he set off and went to his father. But while he was still far off, his father saw him and was filled with compassion; he ran and put his arms around him and kissed him." (NRSV)

Now this father puts his arms around his son before the son can even explain how sorry he is. The son doesn't get a chance to even say, "Father, forgive me. I know what I did was wrong and crazy and disrespectful. I know what I did was stomach-turning. I know what I did was vile." The son never gets a chance to apologize before the father forgives him.

In Luke 23, Jesus has been crucified. His enemies, in addition to other horrendous, hideous acts, have nailed Him to a cross. But look at what Jesus says to His enemies—those who nailed Him to the cross in Luke 23:34: "Then Jesus said, 'Father, forgive them; for they do not know what they are doing.'" (NRSV)

Those who had crucified Jesus hated His guts. They scurrilously attacked Him. But Jesus forgave them. Notice they didn't ask to be forgiven either. They did not ask to be pardoned from the horrible things they had done to Jesus. But He forgave them anyway.

When I was a boy, one day I was walking home and two other boys stopped me and said, "What did you say about my mama?" And I responded, as I turned toward the direction I was going to run, "I didn't say anything about your mama." I kept saying this until I saw where I had a clear opening to run, and then I took off running like a bat out of hell. And I said to those two boys, after I got far enough away and at the bottom of the hill, "I did say something about your mama. She is big and fat and ugly...your mama is so big when she steps on the weight scales it says 'to be continued'...your mama is so big she once went on a seafood diet...whenever she saw food she ate it! Your mama is so big folk exercise by jogging around her!" Boy I went off on them!

A few weeks later, these same two boys showed up at the baseball park. But this time I had them outnumbered. I had my boys with me. There were about fifteen of us, and I could have said "vengeance is mine." But I didn't. They didn't ask—but I forgave the boys; they forgave me too—and I didn't ask.

How do you forgive people? Don't wait for an apology. Don't wait for people to say that they are sorry before you forgive them. It would be good if they did ask for forgiveness. But don't you predicate your forgiveness on whether they do or not. I know someone is saying why should I do that? That's not fair. And I say to you as Mariah Burton Nelson says in her book *The Unburdened Heart* that if you don't it is to your detriment. It will be your own demise that you are plotting.

By deciding to wait on a person to apologize before you forgive them, that could cause you to hang onto anger for years. It could imbue your heart with bitterness and contempt for years. And the other thing that you will be doing is leaving your well-being in someone else's hands. So don't stand around and wait for an apology before you forgive. This is one step in the process of forgiving. There is another step.

## IDENTIFY WITH

Luke 15:22-24 says, "But the father said to his slaves, 'Quickly, bring out a robe—the best one—and put it on him; put a ring on his finger and sandals on his feet. And get the fatted calf and kill it, and let us eat and celebrate; for this son of mine was dead and is alive again; he was lost and is found!' And they began to celebrate." (NRSV)

The question I asked as I read verse 20 was "how could this father so readily put his arms around this son who had wronged him, who had been so selfish and egocentric?" But I knew why when I read verses 22-24. The father said "my son was lost but now he is found." You don't know what it is like to be adrift unless you have been there yourself. You don't know what being lost—confused—is like unless you have been there yourself. And all of us have been lost at one time or another. But we just tend to forget.

This father remembered that he was lost one day. This father remembered that he had not always been who he was. So he understood what his son had done and what his son had gone through in his prodigal living, and what it took for his son to come home. The father identified with his son's struggle.

In Luke 23:34—let me enlarge what the Holy Spirit is transmitting—it says, "Then Jesus said, 'Father, forgive them; for they do not know what they are doing.'"

Jesus could have brought down the angels from heaven to punish His adversaries or even cause the earth to swallow them up, but He doesn't. Why doesn't He do that? Well, our text doesn't say, but I believe that Jesus looked at the crowd who had wronged Him and saw what they were dealing with. There were people in that crowd who were hurting from events that had nothing to do with Jesus. There were people in that crowd that crucified Jesus who had family issues, job issues—who had themselves been abused. So what does Jesus do? He doesn't condemn them; He doesn't denounce them; He doesn't rebuke them. Instead He identifies with them. He has compassion on them.

John 8 correlates with the scripture we just read, but this text brings emphasis to what the Holy Spirit is saying about the other step we need to take in order to forgive others who have wronged us. It says in verses 3-7:

> The scribes and the Pharisees brought a woman who had been caught in adultery; and making her stand before all of

them, they said to him, "Teacher, this woman was caught in the very act of committing adultery. Now in the law Moses commanded us to stone such women. Now what do you say?" They said this to test him, so that they might have some charge to bring against him. Jesus bent down and wrote with his finger on the ground. When they kept on questioning him, he straightened up and said to them, "Let anyone among you who is without sin be the first to throw a stone at her." (NRSV)

This woman was accused of and actually caught sleeping with other men. The scribes wanted to condemn her—the law said they could and they wanted to carry out the law of the land to its fullest extent. But Jesus doesn't do that. Although this woman has done wrong—although this woman has done wrong against God (because anytime we do wrong, we do wrong against our Lord and Savior)—Jesus doesn't condemn her. Instead I believe He identifies with her pain. He identifies with what could have driven her to do such a thing.

There is no good reason to sin, but sometimes our past wounds— our experiences, our idiosyncrasies, things we are dealing with in the present and past—affect our present decisions. Maybe Jesus looked at this woman and said to Himself, "What you did was wrong, but I can see in your eyes that your pain, the agony in your soul, is pushing you in the wrong direction, and you are so desperate for love and affection you have gone down the wrong road." And perhaps Jesus said to Himself as well, "I have never sinned, but I have felt your agony—I understand the torment in your soul."

What am I saying? Empathize with your offender. Someone said that "hurt people hurt people." Sometimes people are in so much agony in their souls that they deal with it by attacking other people. Have you ever seen the play or movie *A Raisin in the Sun* with Esther Rolle playing Mama and Dan Glover playing Walter Lee?

*A Raisin in the Sun* portrays a few weeks in the life of the Youngers, an African-American family living on the South Side of Chicago in the 1950s. When the play opens, the Youngers are about to receive an insurance check for $10,000. This money comes from the deceased Mr. Younger's life insurance policy.

Each of the adult members of the family has an idea as to what he or she would like to do with this money. Mama wants to invest in a house; Walter Lee wants to invest in a liquor store; the daughter wants to invest in an education for herself. Walter Lee eventually takes the $6500 they have left and gives it to a friend to invest in the liquor store, and the friend runs off with the money. His sister says to their mama, "Walter Lee is so stupid." And her Mama grabs her and says to her, "Don't you say that about your brother. You don't know how long he stand up before he went down."

That's empathy. Empathy is the ability to detect not only what others feel but also to experience that emotion yourself. Instead of condemning your offender, being critical and accusing, have you ever thought about empathizing with them? He or she may have acted out of ignorance, fear, or pain, phobia or dread, nervousness, or lack of knowledge—simple naïvete. Mariah Burton Nelson says,

"Behind every jerk, there's a sad story." So it may be that you need to consider empathizing with your offender. You can hate and be filled with rage, but that's going to hurt you more than the person you are furious with.

How do you empathize with others? Think about the stupid things that you have done. You know you are not Mrs. Perfect or Mr. Perfect. You may want people to think that's what you are. But you are not, and in fact none of us is.

The story is told about an old man who died. A wonderful funeral was in progress, and the country preacher talked at length about the good traits of the deceased, what an honest man he was, and what a loving husband and kind father he was. Finally, the widow leaned over and whispered to one of her children, "Go up there and take a look in the coffin and see if that's your pa." (Source: Good Clean Jokes).

You may appear to be perfect and want people to think that you are perfect, but the people who live with you know you are not perfect.

- You have hurt some people in your life too.
- You have done some wrong in your life too.
- You have said some crazy things, been inconsiderate, been selfish in your decisions, and been unkind at times toward others too. So remember that and it will help deflate your stuck-out chest.

106

Remember people make mistakes. All of us will mess up every now and then. There is a song I like by Donnie McClurkin that goes like this:

> We fall down but we get up
>
> We fall down but we get up
>
> For a saint is just a sinner who fell down and got up.
>
> Get back up again. Get back up again. For a saint is just a sinner who fell down and got up.

To empathize with someone who has hurt you, to understand why that person may be so abusive in their words and behavior (and this is not to downplay their behavior and their responsibility for their behavior in any way), remember the words of Donnie McClurkin: People fall down, and they can get up again.

## THINK ABOUT THE RELIEF YOU FELT

But there is something else we can do other than empathizing with the person who has offended us. There is something else we can do besides not waiting on an apology before we forgive. We see the other step to forgiveness in John 4:29.

In this text the Samaritan woman comes to the well and Jesus is there, and they get to talking about various and sundry things. Finally Jesus says, "Where is your husband?" And the woman replies, "I have no husband." And Jesus responds, "You got that right—you have had five husbands, and the man you are living with now is not your husband." Jesus must have gone further in depth with this woman about her background, who she was, what she had done, and what her dreams were because John 4:29 says she took off running saying, "Come see a man who told me everything I have ever done."

Whatever else happened in that conversation between Jesus and this Samaritan woman that is not stated in the text must have lifted her spirit and cleansed her soul. She must have felt that Jesus had forgiven her of all she had done because she didn't run to the town crying "stay away from Jesus!" Instead she cried out in joy, "Come see a man who told me everything I have ever done!" This Samaritan woman felt that whatever wrong she had done—the five husbands, the shacking, and the other things that only God knew—was wiped away. I just get that feel from the text. It does not say that, but you can feel it in the text. This woman had been set free. I guess if the song was out during her time she would have been singing:

Amazing grace, how sweet the sound,

That saved a wretch like me.

I once was lost but now am found,

Was blind, but now I see.

T'was grace that taught my heart to fear.

And grace, my fears relieved.

How precious did that grace appear

The hour I first believed.


Think about the relief you felt when someone forgave you. Think about the load you felt lifted off you when you had done wrong and someone said "I forgive you." Think about how your soul felt fumigated and cleansed when someone said "I forgive you." Nelson says, "It's much more painful to contemplate your own faults and failings than others."

Think about it. How did you feel when you had wronged someone, bruised someone? How did you feel?


- Guilt-ridden?
- Mortified?
- Wishing you could take it back?
- Drained?


If you can feel how you felt when you needed forgiveness, it will definitely move you to want to give forgiveness. I don't know about you, but I felt so thankful; I felt like I had a brand-new day; I felt that what I did I was going to do my best not to do it again.

This prodigal son did wrong. No doubt about it. But when he came to his senses and came home, the father could have been bitter and truculent and scathing. But his father did not use that opportunity to point and shake his finger in his son's face and say, "You no good so and so. After all I've done for you and you treat me like this!" When the boy comes home the father does not use this opportunity to do that, but rather he uses it to simply forgive his son of his wrongdoing. Use the opportunity you have to forgive someone who has wronged you.

- Don't take that unforgiveness in your heart to your grave.
- Don't stand before God with that ugliness in your heart.
- Don't let it harm you any longer.

Use the opportunity you have now to let it go—the boiling rage, the need for revenge, the need to retell the story repeatedly of how that person hurt you.

- It's not doing anything but controlling you.
- It's not doing anything but hampering your destiny.
- It's not doing anything but ruining your beautiful personality.
- It's not doing anything but hurting your relationships with others.
- It's not doing anything but hurting your relationship with God.
- It's not doing anything but making you bitter.
- It's not doing anything but haunting you.
- It's not doing anything but upsetting you.

- It's not doing anything but keeping you locked in the past.

- It's not doing anything but stealing your joy.

So use the opportunity you have to forgive. And I guarantee you will feel much better letting go of it than holding onto it!

# BIBLE STUDIES

# CHAPTER SIX

# GOD'S REMEDY FOR YOUR HURTS

**PRAYER:** Begin this devotion with prayer

**READ THE SCRIPTURE:** John 16:29-33

His disciples said, "Yes, now you are speaking plainly, not in any figure of speech! Now we know that you know all things, and do not need to have anyone question you; by this we believe that you came from God." Jesus answered them, "Do you now believe? The hour is coming, indeed it has come, when you will be scattered, each one to his home, and you will leave me alone. Yet I am not alone because the Father is with me. I have said this to you, so that in me you may have peace. In the world you face persecution. But take courage; I have conquered the world!" (NRSV)

Some time ago, in November 2009, the DC sniper was executed for all the people he killed and critically injured. The DC sniper decided one day that he was going to kill as many people as he could. He hid behind trees and in the trunk of his car with a rifle with a scope on it, and from a distance he shot and killed various people. The families of these victims thought their loved ones were coming home that day but discovered later that they had been shot down in cold blood by a deranged madman. The hurt and pain experienced by these families cannot be put into words.

On another occasion, a military officer killed thirteen and wounded many others. Those families thought their loved ones were safe because they were at home away from the war. But even being at home did not prevent something tragic from happening to them. Words cannot express the hurt and distress these families must have felt.

## DISCUSSION QUESTIONS:

- Why do we hurt each other?
- How do you feel when you are hurting?
- What would you say to these people who are hurting if you had the chance?

In John 16:29-33, let's see what Jesus says about the hurts and pains in this world and what He wants for us:

His disciples said, "Yes, now you are speaking plainly, not in any figure of speech! Now we know that you know all things, and do not need to have anyone question you; by this we believe that you came from God." Jesus answered them, "Do you now believe? The hour is coming, indeed it has come, when you will be scattered, each one to his home, and you will leave me alone. Yet I am not alone because the Father is with me. I have said this to you, so that in me you may have peace. In the world you face persecution. But take courage; I have conquered the world!" (NRSV)

In these verses Jesus sums up all He had told His disciples. With these words He tells His disciples to take courage. In spite of the inevitable struggles they would face, an integral part of what God was saying through Jesus to the disciples was that they would not be alone. Jesus did not want His disciples to be incredulous about this.

He wanted them to understand explicitly that they would face struggles, various trials, and vicissitudes, but they would not be alone. It is as if Jesus says in contemporary lingo, "I don't want these things to happen to you—the hurt, the pain, the struggle—but they are going to happen. They are going to happen to Me, and they are going to happen to you. But just as My Father is with Me, I will be with you."

Matthew 11:28-30 makes it clear-cut what God is saying to us about our hurts: "Come to me all you that are weary, and are carrying heavy burdens, and I will give you rest. Take my yoke upon you, and learn from me; for I am gentle and humble in heart, and you will find rest for your souls. For my yoke is easy and my burden is light."

A yoke is a heavy wooden harness that fits over the shoulders of an ox or oxen. It is attached to a piece of equipment the oxen pull. Jesus relates this story of a person carrying heavy burdens. For you see, a person may be carrying heavy burdens of sin—excessive demands, oppression, or persecution—or weariness in search of God. Jesus doesn't want us carrying those heavy burdens; He doesn't want us hurting like that. So He says come to me and I will free you. I will help you with your hurts.

God doesn't want us to be hurt, but He knows that someday we will be hurt. And so what does He do? He gave us some solutions for our hurts. He gave us some cures for our hurts. Let's explore God's remedy for our hurts. Let's travel through the Bible for a few minutes and see what God's antidotes are for the bruises and bumps we will experience because of the battles we will have in this world.

There are some things we should not do when we are hurt. I want us to look at these, which will lead us to God's cure for our hurt. What is it that we should not do when we are hurting? Psalm 39:2-3 says, "I was silent and still; I held my peace to no avail; my distress grew worse, my heart became hot within me. While I mused, the fire burned; then I spoke with my tongue." (NRSV)

**DISCUSSION QUESTION:** What does this text say to you about what you should not do when you are hurting?

David was hurting and he kept it to himself. He didn't tell anyone. He just kept ignoring it, and his hurt didn't get better—it got worse. Don't ignore it. More than a handful of people have a penchant for ignoring their hurts. When you are hurting, don't ignore it. Someone said, "People think she is strong because she pretends nothing is wrong." Someone else said, "Behind this innocent smile of mine lay words that go unsaid. Words of longing, love, anger, and hate, all repeating inside my head."

Don't pretend like nothing is wrong. Your spouse or significant other says to you, "Baby, what's wrong?" and you say, "Oh, nothing. I'm just fine." But really you are hurting on the inside. Your feelings have been hurt. Someone hurt you on the job, or perhaps at your school, or perhaps at your church. And instead of talking to someone about it, you ignore it.

**DISCUSSION QUESTION:** What are some ways that people try to ignore their hurts? Psalm 39:1 says, "I was silent and still; I held my peace to no avail; my distress grew worse, my heart became hot within me." Ignoring your hurt never heals it.

**DISCUSSION QUESTION:** How do you keep from ignoring the hurt? In John 4:5-18, you see what you can do to keep from ignoring your hurt:

> So he came to a Samaritan city called Sychar, near the plot of ground that Jacob had given to his son Joseph. Jacob's well was there, and Jesus, tired out by his journey, was sitting by the well. It was about noon.

A Samaritan woman came to draw water, and Jesus said to
her, "Give me a drink." (His disciples had gone to the city
to buy food.) The Samaritan woman said to him, "How is it
that you, a Jew, ask a drink of me, a woman of Samaria?"
(Jews do not share things in common with Samaritans.) Jesus
answered her, "If you knew the gift of God, and who it is that
is saying to you, 'Give me a drink', you would have asked
him, and he would have given you living water." The woman
said to him, "Sir, you have no bucket, and the well is deep.
Where do you get that living water? Are you greater than our
ancestor Jacob, who gave us the well, and with his sons and
his flocks drank from it?" Jesus said to her, "Everyone who
drinks of this water will be thirsty again, but those who drink
of the water that I will give them will never be thirsty. The
water that I will give will become in them a spring of water
gushing up to eternal life." The woman said to him, "Sir,
give me this water, so that I may never be thirsty or have to
keep coming here to draw water."

Jesus said to her, "Go, call your husband, and come back."
The woman answered him, "I have no husband." Jesus said
to her, "You are right in saying, 'I have no husband'; for you
have had five husbands, and the one you have now is not
your husband. What you have said is true!" (NRSV)

This woman was a Samaritan, a member of the hated mixed
race, and she had had five husbands and the one she was living with
now was not her husband. This woman had all this baggage she was
carrying. And she came to the well, according to some texts, at the
time she did to avoid people. Why? Perhaps she was ashamed and it
discomfited her to come at any other time.

When she gets to the well, Jesus knows exactly what she needs
and He is candid about it. Is money exactly what she needs? No!

Are clothes exactly what she needs? No! Are shoes exactly what she needs? No! Then what does she need? One of the things she needs most of all is to talk—that's right, to talk. She needs to talk to someone about these issues in her life. She needs to have a conversation about what is hurting her. To keep from ignoring your hurts, talk about them. Sit down with someone you trust—someone you think is wise and has demonstrated this in their life—and talk about your hurts. This is an immutable spiritual principle. This does not change; we need to talk about our hurts.

There is something else besides talking about it that you can do to keep from ignoring the hurt. Matthew 18:15-17 says,

> If another member of the church sins against you, go and point out the fault when the two of you are alone. If the member listens to you, you have regained that one. But if you are not listened to, take one or two others along with you, so that every word may be confirmed by the evidence of two or three witnesses. If the member refuses to listen to them, tell it to the church; and if the offender refuses to listen even to the church, let such a one be to you as a Gentile and a tax-collector. (NRSV)

Jesus does not say the first things we should do when a person has hurt us is get away from them, refuse any contact with that person. He does not say that we should not deal with the person. He says that we shouldn't have anything else to do with the person only after we have tried to meet head-on with them and they refuse to resolve the situation. In this text we just read, Jesus says to deal with the person who is hurting you.

**PRINCIPLE:** To keep from ignoring the hurt, confront the person who is hurting you. Someone said conflict is inevitable, but combat is optional. Confront who is hurting you. Meet with the person—if they are not some wacky nut—who is hurting you or has hurt you and seek a resolution. So one of God's remedies to our hurts is don't ignore them. And the way we do that is we need to talk about them, plus we need to confront the person who is hurting us or has hurt us.

In Job 5:2 we discover something else that God gives us as a remedy for our hurts. Verse 2 says, "Surely vexation kills the fool, and jealousy slays the simple." (NRSV) Underline the word "vexation." In other translations the word may be "worry" or "resentment." Job says that vexation, worry, resentment kills the fool.

In Genesis 15:1 we see these words: "After these things the Word of the Lord came to Abram in a vision, 'Do not be afraid, Abram, I am your shield; your reward will be very great.'" (NRSV)

God tells Abram not to be filled with vexation—worry. Why does He tell Abram not to be filled with vexation or worry? Because God promised to defend Abram ("I am your shield"). And God promised to be Abram's "very great reward."

Psalm 56:4 is the quintessential scripture for the point being made here. We see these words: "In God, whose word I praise; in God I trust; I am not afraid; what can flesh do to me?"

**DISCUSSION QUESTION:** What does that verse say to you? Jesus says in Matthew 10:28, "Do not be afraid of those who kill the body but cannot kill the soul. Instead, we should fear God, who controls this life and the next." Norman Vincent Peale said, "Don't take tomorrow to bed with you."

**PRINCIPLE:** Don't worry about hurts. God's cure to hurts is not to worry about them. Worry won't do anything but bring you down. Worrying about your hurts won't do anything but make you feel worse than you already feel.

**PRINCIPLE:** Worry never solves the problems, it never heals hurt; all it does is increase the size of your pain.

How do we refrain from worrying? Let me show you: Matthew 6:25 says, "Therefore, I tell you, do not worry about your life, what you will eat or what you will drink, or about your body, what you will wear. Is not life more than food, and the body more than clothing."

Now look at verses 32-34: "For it is the Gentiles who strive for all these things; and indeed your Heavenly Father knows that you need all these things. But strive first for the Kingdom of God and his righteousness, and all these things will be given to you as well. So do not worry about tomorrow, for tomorrow will bring worries of its own. Today's trouble is enough for today."

In this passage, Jesus is not saying that food and clothing and other necessities of life are not important. Rather, He knows they are very important but He also knows that worrying about them can easily consume all our thoughts. They really aren't the most salient things. The most salient thing in life is to live as a resident of God's kingdom. Jesus is talking about priorities—the main concern—and He says that when we keep our priorities correct we will not be anxious, worrying about hurts and pains. Some anxieties, some hurts, some vexations are the direct result of having misplaced priorities.

**PRINCIPLE:** To refrain from worry about your hurts, keep a healthy perspective. All of us get hurt at one time or another. But it is not the end of the world. It is not the end of our existence, whether we get over it or not. Tomorrow is coming. The sun is going to rise. So since we know tomorrow is coming, we might as well not allow that person who has hurt us today or in the past to steal our joy and ultimately, if we don't apply this healthy perspective principle, continue hurting us tomorrow.

Keep a healthy perspective. Keep a healthy outlook. You might be hurt right now. But don't go around saying you will never get over it. Don't go around saying you will never bounce back. Because if that is the way you feel, that is the way it will be for you. Keep a healthy perspective.

- Tomorrow you will get better.
- Your days will be bright.
- Your wound will be healed.

God's remedy for our hurts is for us: (1) not to ignore our hurts (2) to talk about our hurts (3) to confront the person who is hurting us or has hurt us (4) not to worry about our hurts (5) and keep a healthy perspective because things will get better if we believe.

# CHAPTER SEVEN

# HOW TO BENEFIT FROM YOUR PROBLEMS

**PRAYER:** Begin this devotion with prayer.

**READ THE SCRIPTURE:** James 1:2-6

My brothers and sisters, whenever you face trials of any kind, consider it nothing but joy, because you know that the testing of your faith produces endurance; and let endurance have its full effect, so that you may be mature and complete, lacking in nothing. If any of you is lacking in wisdom, ask God, who gives to all generously and ungrudgingly, and it will be given you. But ask in faith, never doubting, for the one who doubts is like a wave of the sea, driven and tossed by the wind; (NRSV)

A young man was learning to be a paratrooper. Before his first jump, he was given these instructions: Jump when you are told. Count to ten and pull the rip cord. In the unlikely event your parachute doesn't open, pull the emergency rip cord. When you get down, a truck will be there to take you back to the airport.

The young man memorized these instructions and climbed aboard the plane. The plane climbed to ten thousand feet and the paratroopers began to jump. When the young man was told to jump, he jumped. He then counted to ten and pulled the rip cord. Nothing happened. His chute failed to open. So he pulled the emergency rip cord. Still, nothing happened. No parachute.

"Oh great," said the young man. "And I suppose the truck won't be there when I get down either!"

Life is like this: one problem after another. These continuous problems—expecting one thing and another happens—which the paratrooper dealt with, are typical of life. Problems in this life are not atypical. There is nothing phenomenal about them. There is not one thing unparallel about them. As long as you and I live in this world, troubles will continue to show up.

## DISCUSSION QUESTION(S):

- Why is that? Why do we continue to have problems?
- Why do some people deal with problems better than other people?
- Can prayer solve all of our problems? Why or why not?
- If you had to give someone advice about problems, what would be one or two things you would tell them?

In James 1:2, hear these words: "My brothers and sisters, whenever you face trials of any kind, consider it nothing but joy." (NRSV) I want you to circle the word "whenever." Does "whenever" mean maybe? Does it mean perhaps?

In John 16:33, Jesus says "in the world you face persecution...." (NRSV)

Several years ago I led a mission trip to Jamaica, and on our way back to the airport to come home the truck carrying our luggage had a flat tire in Kingston. We were on the periphery of the airport. We almost missed the plane. When I took another trip, we had an accident in South Africa. While growing up, my mother had a nervous breakdown. While in seminary, my grandmother, who helped to raise me after my mother had a nervous breakdown, died.

Problems are bound to happen. They are certain to happen. We don't like them, and we don't want them, but in this life you will most definitely face problems.

James 1:2 says "whenever."

**DISCUSSION QUESTION:** What else does that one word tell you about problems?

When Ted Kennedy died, everyone thought the election in Massachusetts wasn't going to be a problem for the Democrats to win, but that's not how it turned out. When I took the mission team to Jamaica, we had given ourselves enough time to get to the airport, but we didn't include in that time the unlikely event that the vehicle carrying our luggage would have a flat tire.

Problems are unpredictable. None of us knows when exactly a problem is going to occur. None of us knows when trouble is going to stir up. Things in this world are calm one minute and rocking and rolling and trembling with an earthquake the next.

Look at James 1:2: "My brothers and sisters, whenever you face trials of any kind, consider it nothing but joy." Underline the phrase "any kind." Find a different version of the Bible and underline the word that is used for "any kind" in that translation.

Matthew 12:9-10 says, "He left that place and entered their synagogue; a man was there with a withered hand." (NRSV) In Luke 8:43 it says, "Now there was a woman who had been suffering from hemorrhages for twelve years; and though she spent all she had on physicians, no one could cure her." (NRSV) We have read about a man with a withered hand and a woman with hemorrhages.

Let's look at one more scripture: 2 Samuel 11:1-5 says,

> In the spring of the year, the time when kings go out to battle, David sent Joab with his officers and all Israel with him; they ravaged the Ammonites, and besieged Rabbah. But David remained at Jerusalem.

> It happened, late one afternoon, when David rose from his couch and was walking about on the roof of the king's house, that he saw from the roof a woman bathing; the woman was very beautiful. David sent someone to inquire about the woman. It was reported, "This is Bathsheba daughter of Eliam, the wife of Uriah the Hittite." So David sent messen-

gers to fetch her, and she came to him, and he lay with her. (Now she was purifying herself after her period.) Then she returned to her house. The woman conceived; and she sent and told David, "I am pregnant." (NRSV)

Now we have read about a man with a withered hand, a woman with hemorrhages, and a man who was tempted.

**DISCUSSION QUESTION:** What does this tell you about problems?

Problems come in many varieties and forms. Some are just a sting. And some are rowdy. Others can permeate with destruction. James says whenever you face trials of any kind. *The Message* translation says, "Tests and challenges will come at you from all sides." When we had the flat tire in Jamaica, we did not know what we were going to do. Some people passed us by. Finally a police officer came and stayed with us until help arrived. I learned some lessons from this problem:

- Wherever I am God is with me.
- There are some good people in the world.
- Everyone will not pass you by.

**DISCUSSION QUESTION:** Have you ever had a problem that you learned something from? Take a moment and think about a problem you had that you learned something from, and write it down.

James 1:3 reads, "Because you know that the testing of your faith produces endurance." (NRSV)You know what that says to me? Problems are meaningful. There are some valuable lessons in problems. Problems can be pernicious. They come in various sizes and shapes, but every one of them can produce a better you. This can happen in each and every one of us if we get the lesson that is supposed to come from that particular problem. Problems are significant. They carry great weight. Someone said, "What does not destroy me makes me stronger."

How do you get the benefits or lessons from the problem? I think this is a good question because it helps us to be undaunted whenever a problem raises its ugly head. We see more than just the problem.

## LISTEN

In Hebrews 4:1-2 we hear these words:

> Therefore, while the promise of entering his rest is still open, let us take care that none of you should seem to have failed to reach it. For indeed the good news came to us just as to them; but the message they heard did not benefit them, because they were not united by faith with those who listened. (NRSV)

Some of the Jewish Christians who received this letter may have been on the verge of turning back from their promised rest in Christ, just as the people in Moses' day had turned back from the Promised Land. Notice that those who entered Christ's promise of rest and the

Promised Land that Moses talked about were those who listened to the Word of God with faith. Those who did not cross the threshold into the Promised Land listened to God's Word with reservations.

**PRINCIPLE:** The way you get benefits from your problems is a rudimentary step: listen with faith. Rowland Hill once visited a home and saw a child riding a rocking horse. After watching the boy for some time he wittily remarked, "He reminds me of some Christians. There is plenty of motion but no progress." (The Gospel Herald)

A lot of Christians are not making any progress with their problems. The problems have them rocking, but they're not going anywhere. Say to yourself, "I have this problem, and God is telling me something, and I believe in my heart that whatever it is God is saying to me I am going to understand." If we are going to benefit from our problems, we need to listen with faith.

### WILLINGNESS TO ACCEPT AND IMPLEMENT

Luke 6:49 contains something else that I think will help us benefit from our problems. It reads,

> But the one who hears and does not act is like the man who built a house on the ground without a foundation. When the river burst again, it immediately fell, and great was the ruin of that house. (NRSV)

Listen to this same verse in *The Message* translation:

> If you work the words into your life, you are like a smart carpenter who dug deep and laid the foundation of his house on bedrock. When the river burst its banks and crashed against the house, nothing could shake it; it was built to last. But if you just use my words in Bible studies and don't work them into your life, you are like a dumb carpenter who built a house but skipped the foundation. When the swollen river came crashing in, it collapsed like a house of cards. It was a total loss. (Message)

**PRINCIPLE:** The way you get benefits from your problems is not only to listen but to listen with a willingness to accept what God is saying and implement it in your life. When we don't listen with a willingness to accept what God is saying and implement what He is saying in our life, then our problems get worse. Our situation goes further downhill.

We exacerbate our circumstances; 99 percent of the time we know what God is saying but we don't listen because we want it to be something else. We want it to be another answer. We want it to be the answer we have chosen. We want it to be an unchallenging answer. But if we are going to benefit from our problems, we have to listen with a willingness to accept what God is saying and implement it in our life.

## NEVER TOO LATE

**PRINCIPLE:** Realize it is never too late to make a good choice. It is never too late to make the right decision. Many of us live with regret. I am sorry I'm in debt; I am sorry I didn't finish my degree; I am sorry I didn't save any money; I am sorry I didn't exercise. If you want to get something from the problem—if you want to learn from the problem—then quit living in regret and realize that it is never too late to make a good decision. Start saving money now. Decide to finish school now. Start going to the gym or exercising at home now—it is never too late.

We can benefit from our problems. We don't have to let them beat and defeat us. They can be a bountiful blessing from broken hearts and situations of despair. And the way to do that is to

- Listen with faith. Say to yourself, "I have this problem, and God is telling me something, and I believe in my heart that whatever it is God is saying to me I am going to understand."
- Listen with a willingness to accept what God is saying and implement it in your life.
- Realize it is never too late to make a good choice. Stop living in regret. Regret can hold you back and prevent the most wonderful things from taking place in your life.

# Guideline for Leading a Study of
# *If You Want God to Help You Be at Peace*

I n this book, Derrick R. Rhodes shows how God can help people have peace. To help churches, businesses, community organizations, and individuals facilitate a discussion group, this study guide was developed to help the book be beneficial for all who are looking for peace in their lives. The following are some steps you can use to be successful in your search for peace that passes all understanding:

1.  Give the purpose for the meeting, which is to do a group study of this book.

2.  Allow all participants to introduce themselves.

3.  Hand out the book to all participants before the first meeting so that they can read the Introduction: How to Be at Peace. I would recommend that you not allow the group to be too large because it will hamper full involvement from the total group.

4. In the same meeting where you hand out this book, set a beginning time and ending time for each session, and stick to the time.

5. Begin each session by reading the purpose of each chapter or give your own overview.

6. I would suggest that you read the book first and develop study questions for each chapter. The study questions will be used during your group discussion.

7. In the first meeting also establish the following ground rules:

    a. During the discussion, there are no wrong answers.

    b. The person who has not spoken will be allowed to do so before others who have already spoken are allowed to speak again.

    c. No one should be interrupted unless the leader sees it is time to give someone else an opportunity to speak.

    d. Make it known that all participants are expected to attend all sessions.

    e. There are seven chapters, so the study can last for seven weeks.

8. As the leader, be sure to keep the conversation moving, encourage participation, and thank participants for their answers.

LaVergne, TN USA
23 January 2011
213615LV00004B/1/P